Alfred Charles Beaton

Beaton Ashantees

Their Country History Wars etc.

Alfred Charles Beaton

Beaton Ashantees
Their Country History Wars etc.

ISBN/EAN: 9783337427535

Printed in Europe, USA, Canada, Australia, Japan

Cover: Foto ©ninafisch / pixelio.de

More available books at **www.hansebooks.com**

ASHANTEES:

COUNTRY, HISTORY, WARS, GOVERNMENT,
CUSTOMS, CLIMATE, RELIGION, AND
PRESENT POSITION;

Description of the Neighbouring Territories.

BY

A. C. BEATON.

With Map,

SIR GARNET WOLSELEY, COLONEL HARLEY,
AND OTHER ILLUSTRATIONS.

LONDON:
BLACKWOOD AND CO.,
COURT, PATERNOSTER ROW.

CONTENTS.

CHAPTER I.

Campaign of 1824-26—Sir Charles M'Carthy—Wavering Policy—An interview—Disastrous battle—Death of M'Carthy—Defection of the Fantees and native followers—Another decisive battle—Defeat of the Ashantees 9

CHAPTER II.

The Ashantee Kingdom—Kings—Trade—Customs—Superstitions—Chiefs—The capital—The palace—The King's umbrella—Timbuctoo—Arms—Revenue—The Prah—Fantees 37

CHAPTER III.

Cause of the present war—Lord Derby's opinion—Value of the West Coast Possessions—Captain Maclean—Captain Glover—Native troops—The British force—Sir Garnet Wolseley's artillery—The Gatling guns—Bhootan Campaign—Destruction of Chanah—Towerson, &c. 59

CHAPTER IV.

Palinas—Imports—The Houssas—Major Hume—Kroomen—Sanitary condition of Freetown—Ashantee camp—Coomassie—Produce of the country—Cost of the war—Wealth of King Koffee Calcalli 96

CHAPTER V.

The climate of the Gold Coast—Proper season for campaigning—The Netherlands expedition—Drink for the troops—Hospital accommodation—Extent of Ashantee country and protected territory—Food and shelter—Quettah—Future of Africa 108

CONTENTS.

CHAPTER VI.

The Priesthood—Their influence—Superstition of the natives—Doctors and soothsayers—Herbal knowledge—Unlucky days—Fetish—Occupations, &c. . . 115

CHAPTER VII.

Arrival of the commander and staff—Meeting of Native Kings—Speech of Sir Garnet Wolseley—King of Akim—Present state of affairs. 121

THE ASHANTEES.

CHAPTER I.

Campaign of 1824-26—Sir Charles M'Carthy—Wavering policy—An interview—Disastrous battle—Death of M'Carthy—Defection of the Fantees and native followers—Another decisive battle—Defeat of the Ashantees.

BEFORE proceeding to give an account of the Ashantee Kingdom at the present time, the following description of the campaign during the years 1824-26, will probably be of considerable interest, as the people and general aspect of the country have not materially changed.

In the spring of 1822, Sir Charles M'Carthy, in his capacity of Governor in Chief of the British Settlements on the West Coast of Africa, departed from Sierra Leone for the Gold Coast, in order to take possession of the forts then constructed, which had been given over by the African Company to the British Government. The first visit of Sir Charles was of a short and formal nature:

he read at Cape Coast Castle the
charter and proclamations; guns were
and there were general rejoicings
the natives and foreign residents.
quietude of the country did not
call for a longer stay at that ti
appears that, at that period, the A
demanded and obtained tribute fr
Fantees, although at times resisted;
they treated the inhabitants of Ca
Town and immediate neighbourh
like manner, Sir Charles M'Car
fore departing at the end of his fi
gave orders that he would not ackno
any right on the part of the
Ashantee to make these exactions in
on the residents at Cape Coast Cas
at the same time, it seems to be
ledged that the Ashantee king h
formally given up his claim; and
partly admitted by the British in
made in 1820. The following is
tract from the articles of treaty:—
hereby expressly stipulated that the
of Cape Coast Town, being subjects

King of Ashantee, are excluded from participating in the benefits of either of the treaties, as the king is resolved to eradicate from his dominions the seeds of disobedience and insubordination."

Many quarrels had occurred, and ill-will still existed at the time Sir Charles M'Carthy arrived, and no trade was then being done. It seems certain that the king had forbidden his subjects to do any business at that place; and the natives obeyed him, though many traders passed through the town on their way to the then Dutch settlements. Many fresh troubles arose towards the close of the year 1822, which compelled Sir Charles to return to the Gold Coast.

The following was one of the causes. A mulatto sergeant of the Royal African Corps, stationed in a fort called Aunamaboe, had a quarrel with an Ashantee, and turned him out of the fort. Soon after this, the sergeant above-mentioned was captured by the Ashantees, carried many miles into the interior, and then kept in

irons and bondage. For a long
Ashantees encouraged and circula
port that the then Ashantee ki
Tootoo Quamina, condemned the
was sending back the soldier; b
sequel the king adopted a very
mode of procedure.

He sent a savage into the interi
the sergeant was detained, to put
death, and forward to Coomassie
bone, skull, and the arms of
victim. Sir Charles was now forc
conclusion that he must, in disc
his duty, forthwith punish the pe
of this diabolical act: he, however,
putting his decision into executi
the Fantees should quit the
camp, and arrive in their own pa
knowledged territory. Matters
peared ripe for a surprise and r
justice. Most of the Fantees had
there then remained only an
prince, several captains, and ab
hundred natives. In order to
treachery, the volunteers and

DISASTROUS BATTLE.

Cape Coast Town were called into the fort, and received their ammunition only a short time before the march ; the regular soldiers obtained no notice whatever. A night march and a morning surprise was the mode of action. The distance to be travelled was understood to be but twenty miles ; but the guides were either ignorant or treacherous—perhaps both. The track was lost. In the struggle through the dense bush and swampy marshes the troops became worn out, and were suddenly attacked, and exposed to a very heavy fire from a numerous body of Ashantees and rebel Fantees, ambushed in a dense wood, on both sides of a very narrow, rugged defile. The natives under British control quickly vanished ; but the advanced guard, consisting of a few good men of the 2nd West India Regiment, under the command of the brave Captain Laing, of the Royal African Corps, stuck together, returned the fire, and pushed forward, when, to their grief, they found that they were on the wrong track. Under these circumstances, a general retreat was made for the nearest sea-coast fort, Aunamaboe. By this disastrous affair the British lost one officer and ten men, and about forty men were wounded and missing. There could have been, at this time, but little firmness of purpose among the British authorities on the Gold Coast, for they allowed the matter to rest, with all the honour in the Ashantees' favour.

Sir Charles M'Carthy, it appears, merely contented himself with organising a militia force at Cape Coast Town and neighbouring forts, consisting of picked natives, and, having seen them take the oaths, went off, for a cruise, with Sierra Leone for his destination. During his absence, the Ashantees several times marched over the Prah, and were attacked, with but little result, by a Major Chisholm and Captain Laing.

At this period the Fantees were divided: some aided the British; others sided with the Ashantees. Once, at the capital of a hostile Fantee chief, Captain Laing contrived to surprise an Ashantee camp; but the natives were not only agile enough to escape without loss, but found time enough to kill their prisoners. Nothing definite was done, and subsequently the troops took up their position in two camps, one about thirty miles inland, to the north of Cape Coast Castle, another inland, to the northwest. This position was chosen in order to prevent the Ashantees from proceeding to Elmina and procuring ammunition.

In November, 1823, Sir Charles M'Carthy returned to Cape Coast Castle, and first and foremost devoted his attention to secure the good will of all the chiefs near the Gold Coast, and, as far as practicable, in the interior. Among his numerous dusky visitors at one of the forts, was Appea, King of Adjumacon, who appears to have been capable of acting with good faith, and who brought the whole of his warriors with him. Then ensued a grand palaver, which Appea and chiefs attended with all the state of western chiefs; he himself " reclined on a satin cushion, with a handsomely embroidered cloth of native manufacture to cover his body; his confidential messengers preceded his palanquin, carrying elephants' tails, emblematic of his power, and eight gold-hilted swords; his first wife and sister were in close succession, followed by his bards, who sang his victories and grand titles; his band followed, playing their familiar airs." A few days afterward, Sir Charles walked to a camp a distance of twenty miles, where he was well received by numerous chiefs, who insisted on embracing him. He soon returned to Cape Coast, and remained a short time, in order to complete his arrangements for a methodical campaign against the Ashantees, who were then rapidly advancing to the attack, in fourteen divisions.

On the coast, to the east of Cape Coast Castle, lay a certain Captain Blencarne, in command of a division consisting, for the most part, of native militia, and still less disciplined followings of native chieftains. This division, Blencarne had orders to lead into the interior, with the object of attacking the Ashantee flank and rear.

A similar operation was intrusted to Captain Glover, only that the latter had a more distant base for operations. Captain Laing, with his Fantee troops, was ordered to advance from his encampment into the Assin country, in a direct line between it and Coomassie.

Sir Charles M'Carthy led his own command across the Prah to meet the direct advance of the enemy; Sir Charles took with him the Royal African Colonial Corps, a capital regiment of well drilled and stanch troops, part white and "duskies," all commanded by British officers; a small detachment of the 2nd West India Regiment, and the Cape Coast Militia, natives, badly drilled, and officered by British residents at the forts. Of native allies no numbers are recorded; but early in the year 1824 a force of about 2,500 men had been massed. Sir Charles passed a few days in giving the men bush drill, and a movement on the left bank of the Prah was decided on. At the very outset, the immense difficulties and dangers so often experienced in this country occurred, and checked the progress. "Owing to the difficulty in procuring provisions and shelter, the advance was made in small parties, the carriage of goods alone being no mean obstacle. However, the great mass of his troops were far advanced when Sir Charles heard that the Ashantees had invaded western Wassaw, and the Wassaws were in full retreat. Sir Charles was an unquestionably gallant and experienced officer, and at once made up his mind to cross the Prah with what troops remained, and directed Major Chisholm to take command of the northern force. In most cases one single, crushing blow is what was wanted to settle these barbarians, but the commander had not the requisite number of troops to strike such a blow. The only force with which Sir Charles began to cross the Prah, and so cause the retreat of the Ashantees, consisted of about 100 Gold Coast natives, *new recruits*, three companies of native militia, numbering in all 200 men, and about 250

ANOTHER EXPEDITION. 19

unorganized natives, under their own captains; the latter marched so badly that they were a mere incumbrance. The path lay over precipices and deep swamps; however, the troops commenced crossing the Prah in small canoes, each canoe only holding two passengers at a time; this forming the whole fleet for carrying the men across. Sir Charles landed on the right bank of the Prah, and determined to get into the Wassaw Country. Taking with him the 100 negroes of the Royal African Corps, he set out at once for a twenty miles' march, leaving the rest of the little "army" to follow.

He arrived at Assamacow, and during his stay he heard that the Wassaws and Denkeras were retreating before the Ashantees, and he therefore sent forward an intelligent officer to induce the native tribes, if possible, to make a stand until he could join them.

He also sent to Major Chisholm, and directed him to join him by forced marches. The officer sent forward found the Wassaws and Denkeras in full retreat, and with difficulty induced them to halt. The Governor at once sent forward the regulars and militia, he himself following with the native troops. These men performed many arduous marches through jungles, swamps, heavy rain, and mud reaching above their waists.

The Wassaws had declined to clear the bush for the camp, still less to clear the opposite bank of the river, from where the enemy's attack would probably be made. By-and-by the Wassaws were willing to do the latter; but they were in reality making off with all they could take, when Major Ricketts stopped their way over the river, and set a guard of men to prevent their running away. The Ashantees seldom at that period fought in the night. Shortly afterward Sir Charles M'Carthy came up with his body-guard of 250 men sent him by King Appea, and 50 natives of the Gold Coast; he was also followed by an old chief—so old that he had to be carried in a basket. Sir Charles's native troops had thought proper to stop on the road, and were never afterward seen.

It appears that Sir Charles would not believe that the Ashantees were close on his track, always concluding that the frequent alarms were made to induce him to return. He made up his mind to ascertain how the enemy liked the smell of powder and the attention of bullets. His desire was soon accomplished. On the 22nd of January, 1824, the *real alarm* was given. The Ashantees, numbering over 11,000, came upon the motley and disorganised body under the gallant Governor's " command." The barbarians were well armed with long muskets and long knives; they came running through the woods, blowing horns and beating drums, until within a very short distance, when, making a halt, Sir Charles was induced to believe that a greater part would come over to him; and by way of invitation he made his band strike up "God Save the King." The Ashantees returned the compliment on their musical horns, and the action began by the British and other troops firing across the river at the enemy, who stood on the opposite banks, completely lining the margin of the river.

This scrambling fight scarcely claims the designation of an action. On the side of the British, at the commencement, so far as the soldiers were concerned, there was certainly something like concerted arrangement. The renowned body-guard, acting under the instigation of their chief, took up a position on the left. The Governor repeatedly requested them to alter their position, but all to no purpose. The position was such that no proper formation could have been possible, owing to the dense thickness of the bush, and thus all solidity of frontage was lost. Communication between the men was extremely difficult; indeed, when the combat came to close quarters, it resolved itself into a series of distinct skirmishes. The cowardly Wassaws took the very first opportunity that presented itself of disappearing, as also did the men engaged in transporting the ammunition. Our regulars and militia for several hours kept the Ashantees from crossing the river immediately in their front; but the ammunition becoming exhausted, owing to the desertions of the " carriers " above-mentioned, they were no longer able to hold their own. Sir Charles, in his excitement and anger, blamed the keeper of the powder, &c., for not having ready the requisite supplies and men to act as reserve. No sooner did the Ashantee warriors observe that the fire from our soldiers was slackened than they crossed the river in their front, and by their superior numbers and mode of spreading out their troops in the form of a fan, completely surrounded Sir Charles and his unfortunate comrades in arms.

As might have been expected, the regulars and militia fought as only men can fight under such circumstances; used their bayonets until, through the mere pressure of numbers, they were overcome. No quarter was given, and their heads were immediately cut off. The

Governor had by this time received many poisoned wounds; but seeing that every hope had fled from the centre, he rushed to where the Denkera king was still fighting against overpowering numbers, surrounded by his faithful natives: it was impossible to see many yards around, and therefore hopeless to attempt a retreat.

One small field piece was now used for the first and last time; this appears to have acted rather as a signal to show the position of the British force than as an effective weapon of war, for the Ashantees rushed eagerly forward and despatched the only two men near to Sir Charles, whose last moments had arrived. A Major Ricketts now came up, and, with a few men and Sir Charles, endeavoured to force a way out of the bush. A discharge from the Ashantees sent all the little band back, except Sir Charles, who was never afterward seen.

Major Ricketts and his little band seized a native of Wassaw, who, under fear of instant death, acted as their guide and

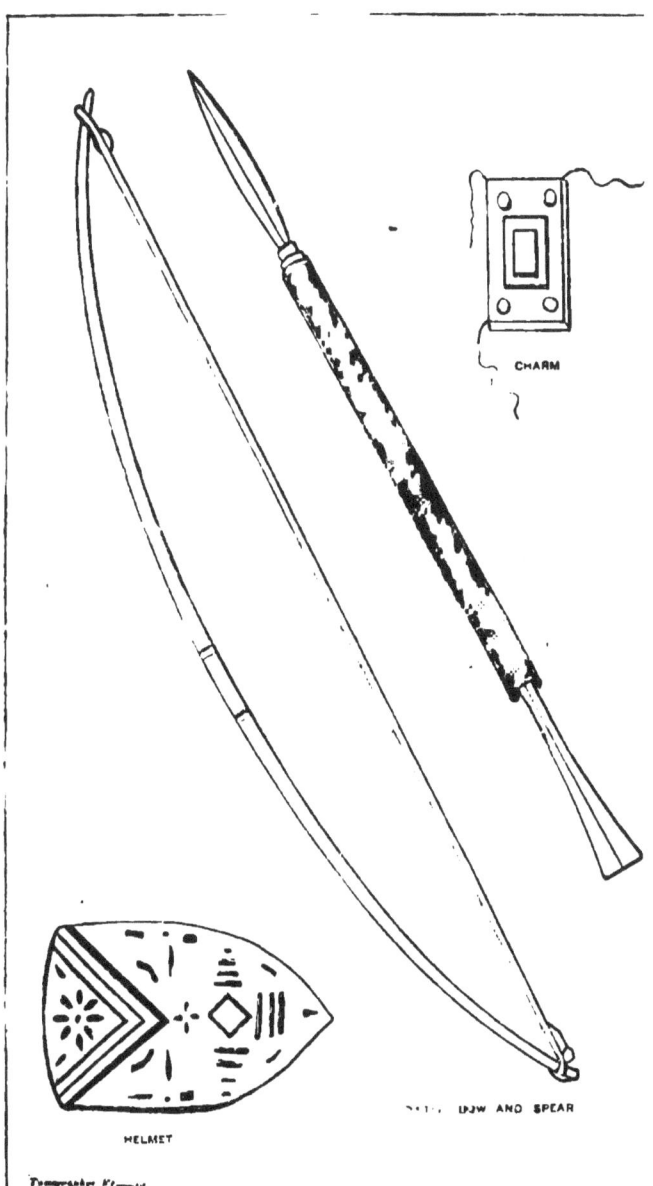

CHARM

BOW AND SPEAR

HELMET

deliverer. Probably enough has been given to the reader to show the position of our troops in this dismal encounter. For the next two days the fugitives proceeded on their way, cutting their own road through the bush, when not hiding from their enemies, and occasionally coming suddenly in sight of the dead bodies of unfortunate men, women, and children belonging to the Wassaw tribe.

After numerous hardships, Major Ricketts and his few remaining men succeeded in reaching Major Chisholm, who had endeavoured to reach Sir Charles M'Carthy, but had met with treachery upon treachery from the natives, and would only have arrived at the scene of action three or four days after the fight was over. These officers, acting wisely, fell back on Cape Coast Castle.

Of the few remaining straggling and wounded wretches, it appears that some reached the coast only to die of hardship and exposure ; others found their way to the land owned by the Dutch ; others to the

c

hostile encampments, to be immediately beheaded.

In the above action nine British officers perished, and about 180 of the regulars and militia disappeared, either having been killed, taken prisoners during the fight, or lost in the woods. No account can be given of the Ashantee loss. It would be a waste of time and space to recount the miserable skirmishes and further marches, suffice it to say all ended in the Ashantees occupying a position close to Cape Coast Castle.

One narrative certainly is worth giving. Certain negotiations for peace passed, in the course of which it was ascertained that the Governor's secretary, Mr. Williams, was still alive, and a prisoner in the camp of the Ashantees. He was brought into Elmina naked, with his hands tied, after having been some months a captive. This officer brought further information as to Sir Charles M'Carthy, to the effect that Mr. Williams had, with two or three others, escaped at the end of the fight with Sir Charles, but the latter was soon afterwards

shot down. His companions removed him
a short distance until they were again
wounded. Mr. Williams was borne sense-
less to the ground, and, on recovering, found
himself in the hands of the Ashantees, some
of whom had recognised him. On looking
round he saw the headless trunks of his
chief and others. He was sent a prisoner
to Assamacow, the place of the Ashantee
encampment, lodged in a kind of shed in
the day, and at night locked in with the
heads of Sir Charles and two officers. Mr.
Williams's diet was as much snail soup as
he could eat, given to him morning and
evening. When the Ashantees cut off the
heads of the prisoners, they compelled this
unfortunate captive to look on at the operation. Some of the prisoners were stripped,
and as they got ill they were put to death.

From the details it seems that it was
the intention of the Ashantees to send
Williams to Coomassie, but did not, owing
to his being wounded and unable to walk.
He was in this condition when his release
was granted. Mr. Williams expressed his

astonishment at the discipline of the barbarians.

In the spring of 1824, the head-quarters of the Ashantees were within twelve miles of Cape Coast Castle. This was the camp formerly occupied by Captain Blencarne and his regular and native troops. More soldiers having arrived from Sierra Leone, Major Chisholm, as the officer now in command, decided to attempt to defeat the Ashantees before their king should arrive with his force of 12,000 men. This experienced and brave officer, with immense labour cut paths through the forest to the position occupied by the enemy, which was on a height, and could command the only paths by which our men could advance. The barbarians made but little show, but pursued their old practice of spreading their troops fan-shape, and attacking the flanks of the British and their allies, but without success. Chisholm's success seemed certain, but the Fantees fled and the carriers of supplies also disappeared. He, however, fought till dark, when want of supplies forced him to fall back as far as the garden belonging to the Government. Again next morning he advanced, only to find himself again deserted by his native followers, with but little exception; a few Gold Coast natives and Denkera natives alone followed him.

It was now necessary for the troops to retire again to the Castle. The Ashantees remained ten miles off, when, on the 29th of May, they were joined by the army under the king of their tribe—not the old and wily King Sai Tootoo Quamina, who died at the capital, Coomassie, at the beginning of the war—but by his brother, Sai Ookoto, who succeeded him. This chief had now arrived on the coast to slaughter and drive the British out of the country, and throw every stone of the Castle into the sea. He deserves credit for energy, for about the end of June he advanced with his army near to the Castle, taking up a position fan-like in form, and extending for about four miles.

Sailors and marines from our men-of-war and ships belonging to merchants, landed, and manned the guns. The miserable Fantee natives, principally women and children, were driven by this advance out of the adjacent towns and villages into the Castle, to the number of about 4,000.

The British were but badly prepared for the attack, the garrison of the Castle numbering less than 400 men, of which number about one-third were patients in the hospital. Deficiency of ammunition is not an unusual occurrence, unfortunately, in our Colonial regiments; and in this case the old leaden roofs of the merchants' houses, old pipes, and anything available were used as a substitute for proper balls and slugs. Added to this, famine made its appearance, in company with small-pox and dysentery, which materially decreased the already small number of devoted men.

A good deal of skirmishing and desultory fighting of the usual character ensued, with but little effect; hunger and disease were, indeed, the principal cause of the barbarians retiring. One of the chiefs belonging to the Fantee tribe made his escape from the Ashantee camp, and informed the British that the enemy were suffering extremely from small-pox and diseases generally, and this, coupled with shortness of provisions, caused the death of thousands, and discontent and desertion, under cover of night, of thousands more. On the 20th of July the Ashantee king fell back on the Fantee provinces, dispersed the residents, and destroyed their villages and cultivated lands. At the same time, hearing that the Queen of Akim intended marching on his capital, the Ashantee king retreated for Coomassie, leaving behind thousands of his wounded, and sick people, who fell into the hands of the returning Fantees, and were soon killed by them. It appears to have been the general belief among the British section that this inroad of the Ashantees would never have been undertaken had they not have been encouraged and supplied with ammunition by the Dutch residents in Elmina. Be this as it may, no authentic information has ever been ascertained.

But little could have happened in this miserable campaign to strike terror into the hearts of the Ashantees, and we are not surprised to find the British again treated to another incursion in 1826. This time the Ashantee ravages appear to have been made in a southern direction, and a most decisive conflict took place about the 20th of September, near British Accra.

The British force then was nominal, but to their aid came our old ally, the King of Denkera, the King of Akemboo, and the Queen of Akim. These three sovereigns contested who should have the honour of a sword-in-hand contest with the Ashantee monarch. The sovereign of Akim is described as having a modulated, cracked voice; and, before the battle, her majesty paraded the lines with her gold-enamelled sword and heavy necklace of leaden bullets; she afterwards appeared in the very hottest part of the fight. However, these three native rivals, having divided the flanks between them, missed their mark, as it is reported the Ashantee king, having learnt the position of the British, determined to make them the centre of his attack. The officer then in supreme command was Lieutenant-Colonel Purdon, who had the Royal African Corps, with natives in the rear. Among others in command was Captain Hingston, who had 600 English, Danish, and natives under his control. From the most reliable information, it seems that the number of our forces was about 12,000, one-third of which number were provided with muskets. The enemy numbered about 11,000, and the most part of the battle was performed with the knife. The British musketeers advanced; the Ashantees gave way, but few prisoners were taken; those that fell were instantly despatched. In this battle the Ashantees fought courageously.

The Danish and Dutch natives ran away in the early part of the action; the Ashantees forced their way, and made the British centre fall back and abandon all advantages hitherto gained; the main purpose of the Ashantee chief being to rout the whites.

At this juncture Colonel Purdon happily arrived, and forthwith advanced with his reserve and their rockets. Many of the rockets were thrown upon the advancing Ashantee army, and occasioned dreadful confusion and distress among them. The Ashantee warriors ascribed the hissing sound and trains of fire to the introduction by the white men of thunder and lightning, invoked from the gods.

On our side the Akemboo king fought desperately, carrying everything before him, gained the camp of the Ashantees, and again attacked the enemy's flank. The grass catching fire as he advanced, marked his progress. The leaders of the Ashantees caused themselves to be blown up; the kind of prairie fire, the rockets, and the activity of the weird forms under the direction of the Queen of Akim, produced a sight of extraordinary strangeness, and suggested the idea of universal chaos. Imagination must, in this instance, supply the place of description, the whole scene resembling some wild fiction or a fairy tale.

Soon the heads of the Ashantee chiefs were brought in, and the fighting ceased. The Ashantees lost at least 6,000 men, including thirty of their principal chiefs. The Ashantee monarch was severely wounded. The British and allies lost 900 killed, and about the same number wounded and missing. No pursuit occurred; the natives on our side turned their attention to plunder, which was general, the whole of the principal camps of the Ashantees being taken. Many hundreds of the Ashantees were taken after the battle and the *loot;* those unhappy wretches were sent to Accra, and sold as slaves. Among the trophies taken by the British was a head, believed to be that of Sir Charles M'Carthy. It was sent to London by Colonel Purdon. From reliable reports, the Ashantee king carried it about with him as a charm, occasionally drinking rum from it. When not used, it was carefully preserved in paper and in a tiger's skin, the latter the emblem of royalty. Some well founded doubts exist as to the skull being the identical one here described. The anticipations indulged in by the British officer then in command, that this complete defeat would be final, have by no means proved correct.

CHAPTER II.

The Ashantee Kingdom—Kings—Trade—Customs—Superstitions—Chiefs—The capital—The palace—The King's umbrella—Timbuctoo—Arms—Revenue—The Prah—Fantees.

WE now direct the attention of our readers to the people of the Ashantee Kingdom— their monarchs, trades, customs, manners, and government.

Koffee Calcalli, the name of the present reigning monarch of the Ashantee Country, is now of the age of 36 or 37, being the eighth king who has reigned over the Ashantees since the death of the renowned Sai Tootoo, who was the founder of the Ashantee Power, and the greatest of their monarchs and fighting chiefs; indeed, this king is the first ruler of whom we have any authentic or reliable record. Previous to his reign, the Ashantees seem to have been merely a tribe similar to the Fantees, struggling with other tribes for supremacy; but about the year 1700, and at the period of the first king's death, they were fast attaining supremacy as a leading power on the West Coast, enjoying a wider dominion than the neighbouring rulers or chiefs.

At the end of several years of continued success in fighting, Sai Tootoo was killed by some of the tribe of Akim, with whom he was always at war, in an action that was fought on a Saturday. By reports, it appears that his death is still kept alive in the memory of the Ashantees, and the most binding oath an Ashantee can take is that now well-known oath, in English meaning, " By Coromantee Saturday," by which is implied that those who disregard the oath may be considered to have no regrets or regard for the death of Sai Tootoo. It is reported that the present Ashantee monarch has taken this oath to drive all English residents out of Elmina and Cape Coast Castle, or to carry on the war for years. Sai Tootoo was succeeded by his brother, Apoo Koo, who, on taking the throne, made fresh attacks on the Akims, and consolidated their territory and his own. The chiefs of the Ashantees then revolted, and this king was compelled to fly, and find a secure retreat in the present capital, the town of Coomassie, from whence he soon after advanced, and fought, and completely routed, the rebellious chiefs.

King Apoo Koo was succeeded by Acquassie, during whose reign there were constant conflicts with the King of Dahomey. This king died about 1756, and was succeeded by Sai Cudjoe. This monarch further extended the Ashantee kingdom, and is regarded now by the Ashantees as the greatest of their monarchs, always excepting Sai Tootoo.

It is during this last named king's reign that we find the first record of the Ashantees in the journals kept at Cape Coast Castle, from which journals it appears that in the year 1766, the Council passed a resolution to observe strict neutrality between the tribes, and especially in the war between the Ashantees and Fantees, at that time going on.

Sai Cudjoe lived to a great age, and at

his death Sai Quamina ascended the throne, he being the fifth of the Ashantee kings. This king remained in power but a short time, being dethroned by a rising caused by his chiefs, and was succeeded by his brother, Sai Tootoo Quamina, who commenced to reign about the year 1802. It was during his reign that the war with the English occurred, described in the foregoing pages. Sai Tootoo Quamina died in the same month that Sir Charles M'Carthy's troops were defeated and himself slain, and was succeeded by his brother, Sai Ookoto, who was the reigning king when the Ashantees were repulsed, and afterwards completely defeated, by Lieutenant-Colonel Purdon, in August, 1826; and the Fantees mark the time of year, and the misery they underwent during the rule of the Ashantees just previous to the above defeat, by calling the time "M'Carthy's Wednesday." Indeed, they make this an oath similar to the Ashantees' oath, "By Coromantee Saturday."

Sai Ookoto was succeeded by Oawedah,

whose death occurred in the autumn of 1867. During this reign further conflicts occurred between the Ashantees and Fantees; but the English troops and the Ashantees never met in war. He was succeeded by the present reigning monarch, King Koffee Calcalli, who ascended his throne in 1867, and is the son of Koffee Tutee, one of the most famous Ashantee chiefs, by Effnah Cobee, who is now the queen mother. Koffee Calcalli is a man of remarkable ability for a barbarian who has not been educated; is of middle height, rather slight figure, wears his beard longer than his chiefs, takes a very active part in the government of the country, and is of a very hospitable nature. Like most of the royal race of the Ashantee Empire, he is of very light colour, his features partaking more of the Moorish than of the Negro type. It seems that nearly all his family, though no mixture of white blood is known to have taken place, are distinguished by the lightness or fairness of their complexion, which is somewhat darker than that of a dark Italian or Spaniard. The reigning king has many wives, the Ashantee laws allowing a monarch any number. His favourite is the Princess Sappon, daughter of the brother of a late king; she is renowned for her beauty, and exercises the greatest influence over her royal husband. About two years ago she bore him a child, which, however, to her great grief, died at an early age. In the kingdom of Ashantee, the queen mother, according to the laws, takes precedence of the wives of the king. She is a person who is considered of greater importance than any of them, and is the only woman who is allowed by their laws to take part in any public proceedings, or have a voice in matters connected with the State. The present queen mother is Effnah Sawab, more commonly known as Effnah Cobee; the first, it appears, is her married, the latter her maiden name. This woman possesses great influence with the king and chiefs, and is remarkable for her shrewdness. This lady can proceed about her business unveiled, although none of the queens can do so; should an Ashantee look on the face of one of the queens when unveiled he is at once beheaded.

The consorts of the king are kept strictly guarded in the "Ladies'" quarter of the royal palace, which building is surrounded with beautiful pleasure-grounds. The guard over the harem consists of eunuchs, called the "King's Eunuch Guard," who number nearly two hundred. The wives of the king are the only women who are not allowed to travel about at their pleasure. The king's chief ministers are Bossumluc Tia and Appiah. These two have the general control of public matters, and possess great influence with their sovereign. There are many other chiefs in his household, some of whom have the care of his domestic arrangements.

The commander of the army which first attacked Cape Coast Castle, and the chief of the force which has recently scourged the Fantee territory, is Amanguah Tia, one of the greatest of the chiefs of the Ashantee tribe, and who owns territories close to the town of Coomassie. This warrior is also entrusted with the governorship of the Bantamnah, which is a large fortified building, and in which are the tombs of the Ashantee kings. The crown and Ashantee treasures are kept in the Bantamnah, which is also the principal storehouse for munitions of war in the Ashantee Kingdom.

The kings of Ashantee always visit it once in every year, and there stop, secluded from the outer world, for twenty-five days.

The Governor of the Bantamnah is forty-two years of age, and is a renowned warrior. In his recent expedition he was accompanied by an aged man, Assa Moquantah, a kind of *Ashantee Von Moltke*. This personage is a little old man, with white hair and beard, and is nearly eighty years of age. This old soldier is looked up to with much devotion, and even affection, by the army, which places considerable reliance on his judgment in war, in which he excels. He was engaged in the second Ashantee war, which has been fully described.

Adumoo is another well known Ashantee leader and chief, occupying somewhat the position of a permanent commander. This individual advises his majesty on most matters connected with the administration of war, and suggests the proper generals to take command in the field; he himself has not had much active service.

Another well known general, noted for his ferocity and cruelty, is Addoo Baffoo. This general commanded the recent Kreepae expedition, which captured several foreigners; among others, four Europeans, supposed to be now in captivity in Coomassie. These prisoners are two German missionaries, a Frenchman, and the wife of one of the German missionaries. Among other chiefs may be mentioned Assaffo Eaggia, Prince of Jabon; Pookoo; and the Prince of Mampon. Among the numerous chiefs, perhaps Eaggia Kessie holds as high rank as any. When the present king entered upon the campaign he assumed the chief leadership, and the chief named Amanguah Tia commanded the rear of the army.

Assa Moquantah is generally with the king, and materially assists in the arrangement of marches, &c. In short, a kind of staff-general. Most of the operations in this war were planned by him, and many of the generals hold subordinate positions to him. The reigning monarch is seldom seen barefooted; he generally wears sandals richly jewelled. When on the march he is carried in a hammock, by carriers. These are generally supplied by one tribe in the remote interior. The king is easily seen to be above all the Ashantees by the richness and magnificence of his attire.

The war dress of the chiefs and king consists of a loose Turkish kind of trousers; easily to be distinguished from the soldiers in the army, who generally wear a tunic and no trousers.

When the Ashantee king left to take the chief command, Assaffo Eaggia, the powerful chief or prince of Jabon, accompanied his royal leader. This prince is the most powerful of all the chiefs, and never enters into any war unless the Ashantee monarch does so in his own person. He brought with him considerable reinforcements of men from his own dominions; indeed, he can, from his own people alone, bring a well armed force of from 16,000 to 19,000 men (most of them warriors) into the field of action. This personage occupies a rank next to the king.

Prince Mampon and Pookoo before described, came directly in his wake, bringing numerous fighting men into the field; each general or chief could probably organise from 9,000 to 11,000 men. The post of leader, chief, or general in the Ashantee army is not always a most desirable position, inasmuch as when the army enters upon a campaign, the general or chief has certain directions to follow, which if not carried out, and the chief returns, he stands an excellent chance of being at once executed; the royal promise is in most instances generally kept. The fatal effect of failure on the person of the generals usually makes them very active and vigorous.

When an Ashantee army is ready to commence warlike operations or to attempt an invasion, and before taking any actual active steps, the general in command sends, by an aide-de-camp, a specification of most of his then demands to the enemy, and two sticks, one short and one long. This means that if his demands are complied with, the war will be but of short duration, and he will be willing to return; but if the enemy refuses, then it will be long and bloody.

A similar method was adopted in the last war with the Ashantees, when Governor Pine commanded at Cape Coast Castle and in the British Possessions.

Coomassie is the capital of the Ashantee Kingdom, although it has not the largest population. It is generally well built, with wide and good open streets. The king's palace is built of quarried stone, consisting of two stories, and is a large and commodious edifice. Most of

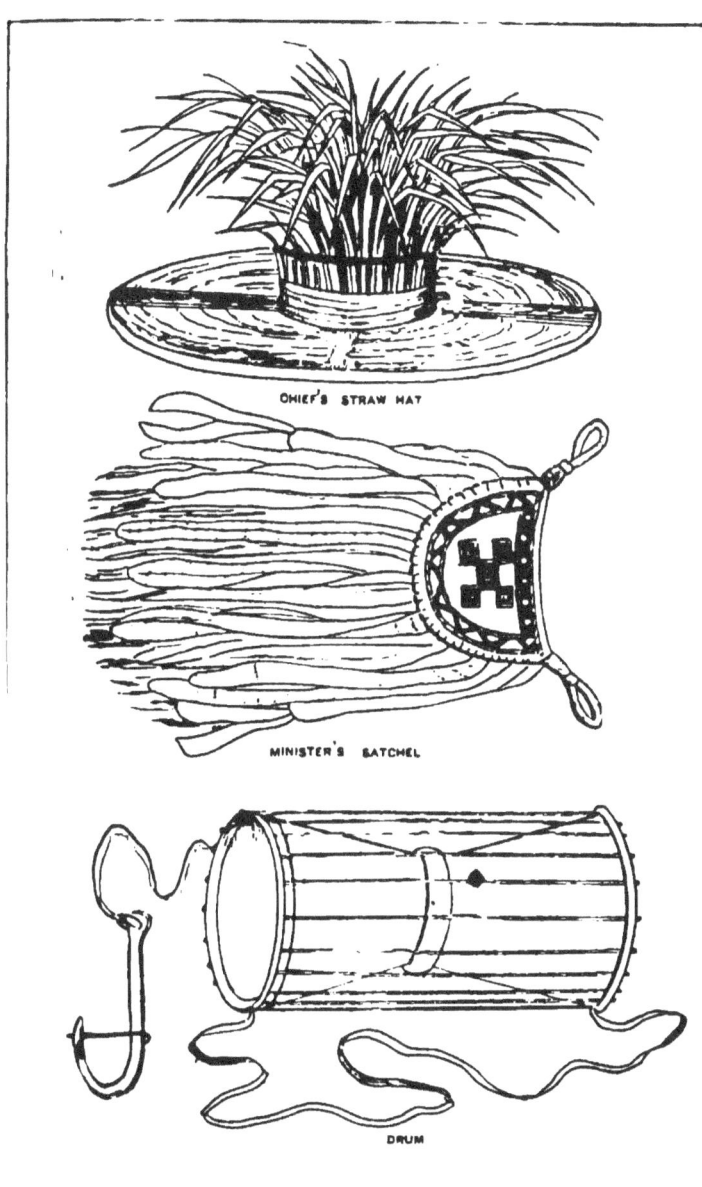

the rooms are very large, and nearly all are lofty. Attached to the palace of the Ashantee kings, is a large court-yard, in which are held the councils between the king, his war generals, counsellors, and the queen mother. The monarch sits on a high throne, the generals and chiefs all around him, those of the highest rank taking precedence. Immediately opposite the king a large space is kept clear, and any speaker wishing to address the assembly mounts a low throne, and stands while speaking.

The principal buildings in the capital are the palace and the Bantamnah. The principal streets, or, speaking more correctly, principal squares, are Market Square and Cannon Square, the latter taking its title from a trophy of three useless cannons standing in it, which report says were taken from the Dutch many years ago. In Cannon Square the king gives state receptions and public audiences to his faithful subjects. The population of Coomassie is about 40,000. Probably the most populous town in the Ashantee dominions is Salaga, the capital of that part of the western coast and interior held by the Prince of Jabon, who has been already mentioned. This last-named town has long been famous for its first-class breed of horses, and is situated on the Upper Volta, about 215 miles from the town and capital, Coomassie. A most extensive trade in cloth is carried on at Coomassie; this cloth is very durable and fine in texture.

When an Ashantee army sets forth for war, few banners and flags are displayed, and it seems that these barbarians attach but very little regard or honour to flags; it would, however, appear that umbrellas belonging to the generals, chiefs, and king, claim the honour usually given by civilized nations to flags. When at war the king's presence can easily be discovered by observing the state umbrella, which is always carried near to or over him by one or two of his favoured chiefs. The umbrella bearer must be a man who has been very victorious in war, and one that holds the first rank. The umbrella belonging to the king is of enormous size and is constructed of blue and red velvet, most laboriously covered with gold and silken ornaments. In order to give the reader an idea of the value of these umbrellas, it may be added that one belonging to a chief of the first rank costs about £300. The state war dress of the King of Ashantee consists of a light tunic of blue velvet or kind of damask, reaching to his waist, light and loose trousers of similar stuffs, ornamented with gold; he wears a cap of blue or red velvet, or cloth, worn in the form of a turban, all embroidered with gold.

Timbuctoo supplies the ornaments and velvet used by the kings, and also the chiefs' umbrellas and clothes. Timbuctoo is in the interior of the country, and it would seem, from reliable reports received from travellers and released prisoners, that the Ashantees are not quite dependent on the supply of ammunition from the coast, but obtain it through Timbuctoo and adjacent places. The greatest disgrace that could happen to the Ashantee army would be the loss of the king's umbrella, and should a chief be so unfortunate as to lose his, he would be a long time before he could retrieve his lost honour. According to the rank of the chiefs are their umbrellas ornamented, so that those holding positions next the king have very costly and splendid ones, although none are equal to the size of his majesty's, nor are any allowed to have the same shape, or exactly the same colours.

When in the field, the arms carried by the Ashantees are long muskets, the length of the barrels being about 5 feet 6 inches. The warriors are also called Buccaneers, and these soldiers also wear in a girdle or sash long and large pear-shaped knives, which in hand-to-hand conflicts prove to be very effective and destructive weapons. The powder is carried in a long leather case, and the bullets, slugs, or pieces of metal are carried in matted bags. About one-sixth of the army are armed with short carbines or blunderbusses, which are loaded with several bullets, slugs, or pieces of iron at a time; and about one-fourth of the Ashantee fighting men carry a long pike between 5 and 6 feet long. The manner of raising the Ashantee army is similar, in some respects, to the course adopted in our early English times. Many of the principal generals command a distinct body of their own serfs or subjects. The regiment, division, or company, or whatever term will best describe the sub-divisions of the army of these savages, consists of the men brought to battle by the lesser chiefs, who are placed under the command of one of the principal chiefs. As in European countries, the different regiments are distinguished by the different colours of their dress and caps, and each chief has to supply his own men with food, although the minister of war supplies from the king's revenues all extra and necessary food.

The revenues of the King of Ashantee are derived from his gold mines. He owns all the principal mines as his private property, by right of accession to the throne. Moreover, every nugget of gold found belongs to him, the person finding the nuggets being allowed only to take the dust as his share. By some accounts, it appears that the Ashantee crown descends in the line of the females, the sons of the king's eldest sister taking power in turn; but it appears that all the Ashantees place great stress on having the blood of the renowned Sai Tootoo in the sons of their kings. The present king's heir-apparent is the Prince Menoh, and the next, allowing the above information to be correct, would be Ana Quassiah.

The capital of the Ashantee Kingdom, namely, the town of Coomassie, is nearly 145 English miles inland from the Cape Coast; it is an open and quite unprotected town. The chief difficulty in an expedition to Coomassie would be the passage of a range of hills known as the Andansee Hills. These hills are very precipitous a very few miles beyond the Prah, are covered with an almost impenetrable bush, and are now only passable by paths sufficient for two or three men to walk abreast, so that here rockets, Gatling guns, or field-pieces would be of but little use, and, moreover, as is well known, the Ashantees are capital bush fighters. This bush is very dense nearly the whole distance from Cape Coast; the country, beyond the Prah, is easily traversed by very fair roads, and up to the time of this last Ashantee outbreak, was studded here and there with neat towns and villages. The Prah, which divides the territories of the Ashantees and Fantees, is but a small stream, and in the dry season has about two feet of water in depth, and is but a very few yards in width. The English troops have been as far as its banks, but no authentic report can be found of their having crossed it. Undoubtedly the chief obstacle to be dealt with is the climate, which, without question, is the most to be dreaded. Campaigning out in the damp bush for only a few nights would prove to have more terrors for the European troops than any possible encounter with the Ashantees. Whatever renown a military man may have for skill in fighting, anything like heavy operations in the open field in all seasons is next to an impossibility. The dry season of the year is about the middle of the month of November, but great difficulty will soon be experienced in providing the necessary baggage and supply of food for anything like an effective force of men. Near the British settlements no horses or other beasts of burden are to be found, and the chief carriers are the native porters, who must have pretty strong necks, for they carry everything on their heads, and, as in the case of some work recently done on the coast, they would, if a wheelbarrow were given them, carry that article on their heads rather than wheel it or use it in a proper manner.

The Ashantees wear very large beards, and are thus easily to be distinguished from the neighbouring tribes. Every Ashantee has at least a short pointed beard, and a beardless Ashantee is reckoned

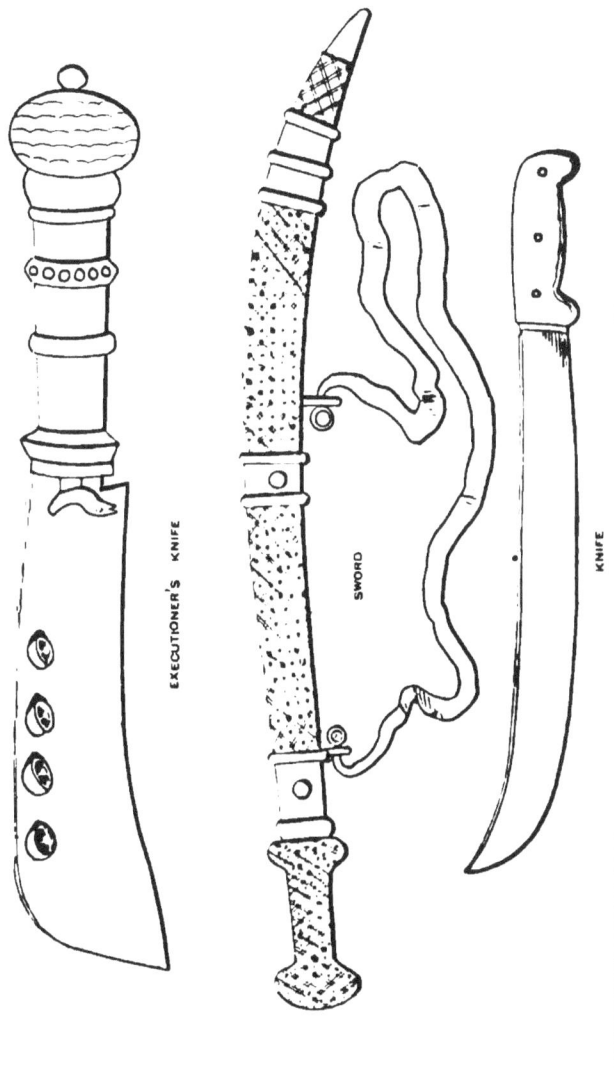

as unfit for a warrior; the appearance of an Ashantee warrior may be considered as fierce, and they possess a natural dignity of character and demeanour.

The tradition in the two nations as to the origin of the names Fantees and Ashantees is that the names are derived from two shrubs, Fan and Shan. The former people, in ancient times, existed almost exclusively on the root of the Fan, the latter finding material support in the root of the Shan, although each nation believes that it came from one common stock, and that the people are only divided by former wars and petty jealousies. It may be stated that on the coasts of Africa the Ashantees are spoken of as Shantees, and the Fantees by the name of Fantees or Faneatees.

As in other countries, the king occasionally proceeds with some state to hunt, although he does not proceed far, as there is but little game or animals of any description in the country. Justice is administered by the king, assisted by one or more of his chiefs, sitting in solemn state, and generally attended by the queen mother and princes. The natives state their troubles and call their witnesses; all are examined by the king and chiefs, who afterwards retire to consult, and then give final judgment.

The Ashantee king, it is believed, can bring into warfare and offensive operations an armed force of upwards of 150,000 men. Should his capital or near territories be invaded by Europeans, he would nearly double his number of fighting savages, most of whom would then act on the defensive only. But it should be borne in mind that the Ashantee kings seldom take the lead of their armies, except when they put forth all their strength, and then they are invariably supported and much strengthened by the addition of their chiefs and their armies.

CHAPTER III.

Cause of the present war—Lord Derby's opinion—Value of the West Coast possessions—Captain Maclean—Captain Glover—Native troops—The British force—Sir Garnet Wolseley's artillery—The Gatling guns—Bhootan campaign—Destruction of Chanah—Towerson, &c.

It appears to be generally understood that the cause of the present war was that one of the chiefs of the Ashantees carried off into the country of the Fantees a certain quantity of gold belonging to the Ashantee monarch, who forthwith sent a messenger to the Fantee chiefs demanding the fugitive and the gold. This demand was not complied with; although, if it had been, the savage would most certainly have been killed. It must appear clear to the reader that the British ought not to have countenanced this breach of faith on the part of the Fantees.

It is probable that, in dealing with African barbarians, we shall not easily learn the lessons of experience; and it would appear that, in the late war, the English relied too much on native help; and the English people are again promised the same kind of assistance from the Fantees, Denkeras, and Wassaws; and, further, that an open rebellion on the part of the Ashantee chiefs may be expected shortly. Such aid, if accepted, should be dealt with very cautiously, and little reliance placed upon it. It must, however, be borne in mind that the work to be done is surrounded with no ordinary peril: there are numerous known dangers, as well as unknown chances in the fortunes of war.

It is apparent that this war was entered upon without any proper knowledge of the rights of the Ashantees, and without proper calculation as to its difficulties generally; and we cannot do better than quote part of a speech recently made by Lord Derby—

"The liability to quarrels of this kind is one of the penalties we pay for extended empire; and as long as we have an enemy in our front, although that enemy should be only a Gold Coast savage, there will be no difference of opinion among politicians of all colours as to the necessity of defending British territory, or of vindicating our honour by resenting attack. That may or may not be an easy business. I don't venture to prophesy. I believe that in Sir Garnet Wolseley we have an able and energetic commander; but neither courage nor skill is proof against disease, and improved artillery won't help us where the chief enemy we have to fight is fever. It is a doctors' war and an engineers' war quite as much as a soldiers' war. Let us keep our men healthy, and make roads they can travel on, and all the black fellows in Africa won't stop them. But it is impossible not to see that those are two conditions on the realisation of which you can't reckon with safety; and if a disaster should occur, we must be so far prepared for it as not to exaggerate its real importance, and to break into a wild freak of indignation against everybody concerned, without waiting to hear what they have to say for themselves. When the necessity of defence is provided for, there will be two other points to consider: first, how we got into the quarrel, and who is responsible for it, which, of course, is not a question to be raised here, even if my own judgment were more fully formed upon it than it is.

" Next—and in the public interest it is a much more important matter—we must make up our minds as to what we are to do to prevent such troubles from breaking out again. Now, on that matter I have a very decided opinion. I trust that no visionary ideas of a vast tropical empire in Africa— no exaggerated fancies as to its being our duty to put a coat of moral whitewash on every black man we come across, will lead us to extend still further a protectorate which, I hold, had better not have been allowed to reach its present dimensions. I doubt whether it was wise to take over the Dutch forts; and I greatly doubt whether any man, in or out of the Colonial Office, exactly knows, or could define, the limits of our authority and of our responsibility in regard to tribes included within the protected territory. No doubt, pledges must be kept, but the narrower the limits within which we contract our relations with those tribes, the better, I believe, it will be. I have no great faith in that kind of moral influence which you acquire by burning a man's house over his head, and telling him he is to be your subject, whether he like it or not. I believe, as a matter of fact, that trade is found to grow quite as fast, if not rather faster, in places where we do not exercise political power than in those where we do; and while I firmly believe in the value to the Empire of colonies to which our own people can go out, and where they can work, I think, to put the thing plainly, that we have got black men enough, and that we had better not go in for more."

The primary object to be gained by the present war is, after all, sufficiently plain. The Ashantee king, after ravaging the territories now on friendly terms with the English, most certainly attacked our soldiers in their principal fort, and put them in a position of extreme danger. Unless we were willing to throw up our possessions on the Gold Coast, it was necessary to act at once on the offensive, thoroughly defeat the Ashantees, and so obtain some probability of future security for the establishment of solid peace on that coast: in plain words, to fight or run.

What are the nature and the worth of the British possessions on the West Coast of Africa? Out of the whole of the possessions on the coast, the Gold Coast is probably the worst. No cattle live long in the unhealthy climate. Certainly, the majority of the Englishmen do not die there, but they are invalided home, only to find their days shortened by the exposure they have undergone. They die, and leave behind them helpless wives and children. Perhaps it would be best, should it ever be found to be practicable, to keep a native force officered by native men in a country so deadly to an European constitution. Ever since the slave trade was given up by England, in the beginning of the present century, the principal reasons for keeping up the settlements on the West Coast of Africa have been to prevent all future efforts to re-establish the trade in human flesh, the encouragement of British commercial enterprise, and the proper protection of the interests of traders. It is a fact that no foreign nation imports negroes from the Gold Coast: therefore the slave trade may safely be pronounced as having become completely extinct. The results from trading on the Gold Coast are by no means to be despised, for in the year 1871 the British exports were about £477,000, and the imports about £399,700. It is not very satisfactory to find that even these figures do not compare favourably with the results of British trading on coasts not subject to European rule and European military government. No doubt merchants like to feel protected, by trading under the protection of British officers and British troops, but they certainly appear from statistics to do a larger trade without this protection.

Formerly the Gold Coast was under the

management of a commercial company, headed by Captain Maclean, a man of vigour and integrity, and who exercised great power over the African savages. In 1824, as we have seen, the Ashantee king gained the upper hand, and it was nearly three years before a patched-up peace was entered into with that monarch; then, again, nine years ago, the Fantees, our allies, committed slight depredations on the Ashantee territories, which resulted in the Ashantee king ravaging the territory of the Fantees at pleasure. Our influence in times of peace over the Ashantees is not great, and as to the Fantees, many are discontented, and have little belief in our protective power.

It is a question whether even at an expenditure of millions a permanent power can be maintained on this coast, and from the statistics already alluded to, the trade appears to thrive as well without as with military protection. On March 8th, 1870, Mr. Cardwell said, "Having made large reductions in the Colonies, the question naturally arises, are we giving the benefit of them to the British tax-payer; because if we are to do so we must reduce the number of men on the face of the estimates. What we propose to do is to disband the Canadian Rifles, the Cape Mounted Rifles, the 3rd West India Regiment, and the African Artillery. And can anybody think that it is expedient that we should continue to pay the expense of these Colonial corps?" After giving his reasons for disbanding the Canadian and Cape Rifles (which we have not now under consideration), he said: "We had a much more pleasant reason for discontinuing the services of the 3rd West India Regiment. When I first went to the Colonial Office, I found two West India regiments quartered on the West Coast of Africa. These two West India regiments were not considered sufficient for the duties they had to discharge, and there was a continual pressure for an additional force. However, the seat of the government of the Colonies on the West Coast of Africa was changed. One governor from

Sierra Leone now superintends the whole of these Colonies. This gentleman was in London last October, and my noble friend, the Colonial Secretary, and I had the pleasure of hearing from his lips that what two regiments could not do two years ago two companies were perfectly competent to do now, and that, except for a temporary interruption of tranquillity between the Dutch and some of the Blacks in one of the settlements, which required the presence of two companies more for a short period, he would be quite content with two companies at Sierra Leone." Again, in 1871, Mr. Cardwell said, " I contend that when we disbanded the Canadian Rifles, we did nothing to impair the defensive power of England, nor did we do anything to diminish that power when we disbanded the Cape Rifles. The same remark may apply to the West India Regiments and to the black troops on the West Coast of Africa, *neither of whom afforded any source of strength to England*. These disbandings lightened the burden of the British tax-payer, while they in no respect diminished the power and influence of this country."

One of our best and most experienced officers now in Cape Coast territory is Captain John Hawley Glover, who is also assisted by other officers, selected on account of their experience in African life and warfare. Captain Glover (who is called the father of all the Houssas) will first of all land at Accra, and will then proceed to the entrance of the River Volta, where he will form a depôt. It is anticipated that he will be accompanied by a very small force of Houssas, although he will have 4,000 stand of arms of a superior make to any possessed by the Ashantees, and he will doubtless act with great caution as to which tribe he entrusts with the best firearms, considering that it is not improbable but they may behave treacherously at no very distant period. This gentleman recently purchased some horses, and as the country round about Accra and Addah is principally grass-land, it is anticipated that these horses will live, although it is a positive fact that in no other parts of the Gold Coast will they live. He has also chartered a small steamer, called *The Lady of the Lake*, which he intends to use in navigating the River Volta, up which river he anticipates he will be able to proceed with this steamer (which only draws about four feet of water) nearly 100 miles. Captain Glover's expedition requires no little courage and enterprise from all concerned, considering they are proceeding, almost without protection, fifty miles from the English garrison at Accra, and this garrison consists of only about 50 men. On all sides the country is inhabited by savages, whose allegiance is of a very uncertain nature; and in the face of all these slender advantages, he anticipates raising a force, within three months, which will, in all probability, be required to enter into conflicts with a force many times its superior in numbers.

Captain Glover's force will attack a country never before seen by an European. To do this, he relies on his influence with some of the native tribes, such as the Akims and Accras, who are considered the best warriors of all the Fantee tribes. Captain Glover bears the character of being a stern but just leader, and has always met with most extraordinary success, and obtained influence over the native troops hitherto under his experienced command. From the last accounts it appears pretty certain that the Ashantees are masters of most of the country to the west of Elmina. The present British force being scattered in small numbers throughout a vast extent of country, and as it appears to be but of little service, either for offensive or defensive operations, it is certain that the termination of the present war will have to be carried up to Coomassie. The recent inactivity of the English force is very acceptable to the Ashantees, who, latterly, have not shown themselves on the open so much as formerly.

Redoubts and fortified posts on the bank will be at once extended, most of which will be formed on the direct route to Coomassie. These forts will be erected principally by Fantees, protected by either English soldiers or Houssas. It would have been best if the Government had had sufficient acclimatized troops on the West Coast at the outbreak of the war to direct native labour, as new troops soon succumb, under the influence of the sun, malaria, mosquitoes, and spirits. Floating hospitals have been prepared, but it would be far better if a sanatorium be formed at Victoria, or the nearest healthy place. Hundreds of hearty and strong men will be killed by their want of knowledge of how to live in this detestable climate.

It will be admitted that most modern battles have been won more by skill in campaigning, artillery, and engineering, than by personal bravery; and it has been seen that the country of the Ashantees consists of thick jungles and narrow paths, in lieu of roads. As horses or bullocks cannot be used, we fall back to manual labour. The following is a description of Sir Garnet Wolseley's artillery from the official reports:—

SIR GARNET WOLSELEY.

"It would have been manifestly absurd to send out 9-pounder or 16-pounder field guns, which could not move up the country without some species of four-footed traction, yet it was necessary that some artillery should be supplied to the expedition. In mountainous countries it is necessary to employ very light guns, and these guns are carried on the backs of mules, or on carriages that can be drawn by the men. Sir Garnet Wolseley will take artillery into the field of the above nature. He will have one or two batteries of 7-pounder rifled guns, about four guns in a battery; also a battery of small smooth-bore howitzers, a few Gatling guns, and 9-pounder Hall rockets. His infantry will be armed with breech-loading Sniders, the irregular forces with muzzle-loading Enfield rifles and smooth-bore muskets. The 7-pounder gun is the smallest rifled gun. It is a muzzle-loader, made of steel; is 150 lb. in weight, has a calibre of 3 inches, and fires a charge of 6 ounces. This little gun is, however, formidable; it throws

F

a shell of 7 pounds, containing a bursting charge of 7 ounces. Shrapnell shells can also be used with this handy gun, and these shells were used with deadly effect in the Abyssinian War. It also fires case-shot, for close quarters, and a light-ball or "star" shell, to illuminate the country, and thus show the exact position of an enemy on a night however dark.

"The smooth-bore howitzer is not so good, either as regards lightness or power, as the rifled one; but will be of good service in the hands of the least trained part of the army. This weapon is made of bronze; is 230 lb. in weight, has a calibre of 4·52 inches, and fires a charge of 8 ounces. It throws a spherical common shell weighing 8 pounds, and holding a bursting charge of 6 ounces; it is also provided with a spherical Shrapnell shell, which, however, is but of little use, except at very close ranges. Probably the last-named weapon will be given out to the artillery branch of that part of the army in which the native infantry are to be provided with old flint-lock muskets, in accordance with Captain Glover's instructions, ho, who doubt, knows the proper weapon for these men. The carriages for the 4½-inch smooth-bore howitzers are of the same make as those for the 7-pounders, being manufactured of wrought iron, with 3 feet wheels, and 2 feet 4 inch track. The Gatling guns will be mounted on similar carriages, as these are intended for the defence of stockades. The Gatling guns are of no use for bush fighting, but can be handled with great effect in any of the few chances that may occur of fightin the enemy in the open. When well handled, the gun is very effective at from 500 to 600 yards. It consists of ten barrels in connection with a grooved carrier and lock-cylinder, well secured on a main shaft. Each barrel has its lock; so there are ten locks to a gun. The locks work in holes in the lock-cylinder, on a line with the axis of the barrels. The lock-cylinder, which contains the locks, is surrounded by a casing, which is fastened to a frame on which are the trunnions of the gun. Immediately over the chambers of the barrels is a description of hopper, through which the cartridges are fed from a drum. Lastly, in the rear is a handle, like the handle of a street organ, which works a crank, and thus drives the whole apparatus. By *merely working the handle*, all the barrs, with their respective locks, are made to revolve; the locks are also made to move backward and forward in their sockets, and are cocked and fired. When a cartridge drops through the hopper, it falls into a groove in front of one of the chambers; as the handle revolves a lock comes forward, and pushes the cartridge into the chamber of the barrel, at the same time slipping the extractor, which is attached to the lock, over the rim in the base of the cartridge case. As the handle further goes round, the piston of the lock is successively cocked and released, thus firing the cartridge, and the lock finally withdraws itself and extracts the empty case. In this way, five of the locks and barrels are constantly performing some of the operations of loading and firing, while the other five are extracting the empty cases; and it is clear that so long as cartridges are dropped into the hopper, and the handle is in motion, the firing will continue, so that a perfect rain of bullets may issue from the ten muzzles. This gun is also provided with an arrangement by which a traversing motion may be given to the barrels while the firing continues; it would be ridiculous to constantly fire a Gatling gun in only one direction. But very few men (those directly in front) would be completely perforated, while it is obvious that those on the flanks would escape; but by the traversing arrangement the enemy generally would be subject to a heavy rain of bullets. This formidable weapon would be perfectly useless in many situations. Should the enemy be in the bush, the rifled guns would be used, and not Gatlings. The present campaign is one in which the most deadly foe will doubtless prove to be the climate, and it is very satisfactory to learn that every precaution will be taken both for the provision of proper medical necessaries as well as weapons of war: generally the preparations are ample.

During the campaign known as the Bhootan Campaign, the howitzers, which formed part of the expedition, had to be carried on elephants, in consequence of their being too heavy for mules; but when slung on a pole they could not be carried along a narrow mountainous or other path by two men, so that they actually became a burden and impediment to a rapidly moving force, whether advancing or retreating; indeed, so much of an impediment that a half-battery of them had to be left behind at a place called Dewangiri. As before stated, the howitzers were carried on elephants. Two were hung on either side of the elephant, on whose back was a kind of saddle made for the purpose; the carriages belonging to the guns were placed on the back of another elephant, and the wheels hung at the sides of the same beast. The ammunition, say 100 rounds per gun, packed in loads, was carried upon the backs of other elephants, but was far too cumbrous for carriage by mules, coolies, or by any ordinary method, when travelling by difficult and narrow defiles, or mountain paths. However, on the Gold Coast the largest quadruped is acknowledged to be a goat—elephants being, therefore, out of all question; although, presuming that elephants might be exported to that country, and could live in the bad climate, they certainly might be utilized to convey many descriptions of guns and munitions of war. It appears that the Rifled Mountain Train formed and used for service in Abyssinia, had the following advantages :—the general equipment was light and very portable under the most difficult conditions. The guns were also powerful and accurate, and could be used either as mortars or guns—in other words, for both vertical and horizontal fire.

The difference between the Rifled Mountain Train for Abyssinia and that for Ashantee is that the Ashantee Mountain Train will be constructed for man-draught instead of mule-draught. This gun will be mounted on a small iron carriage, which will be fixed to a limber furnished with a pole, and to this pole the natives will be harnessed. The carriages are made so that the guns can be used for either vertical or horizontal fire. When the guns are fired at high angles, they can either be fired in the ordinary manner, or the wheels can be removed, and then the gun fired on its carriage, resting directly on the ground.

The principal trying duties of the engineers will be in connexion with these handy mountain guns in the war with the Ashantees. A careful selection of the ground from which the fire of the guns will produce the *greatest* effect, with the *least* hazard of capture by surprise, will be required; the proper care of the ammunition stores, and the careful handling and general working of the guns are of no mean importance.

When artillery is used in a country abounding with bush, and where the enemy can steal near without being seen, the utmost care is necessary to secure the protection of a goodly number of infantry. The selection of the ground is more difficult, as it is not always optional. Again, in a very bad climate, like the Ashantee Territory, considerable deterioration in the value of the munition and stores may be counted on with certainty.

Former failures will make the English public watch with great interest the proceedings of Captain Glover and his soldiers, as it is evident their task is not light. A mere handful of Englishmen, with but few Houssas, have proceeded up a country, surrounded by very doubtful friends and many open enemies, and their intention is to raise a large number of natives as soldiers, and take the field against the Ashantees, who will far outnumber them. The leader of this expedition has had considerable experience, and is, as before stated, well known to have great ascendancy over Africans, so much so, that he is generally called " The

Father of the Houssas." His task cannot be accomplished speedily, and from information it appears that he has allowed himself about three months to discipline his recruits and followers; and if this can be done, he is the man who will do it. The Fantees have proved to be very inferior in fighting capabilities to the Ashantees, so that the Captain has not very good materials to go to work with. The reader will doubtless, however, recollect what talented officers made in the way of soldiers in the case of the Sepoys, and also the wonderful career of "Chinese Gordon" at the head of the Chinese troops; and, as it has been found practicable to make good soldiers out of Hindoos and Chinese, probably the same can be done with the Fantees. One of the many reasons why it would be very beneficial to employ native troops is that they would be, in a great measure, proof against nearly all the dangers which prove to be very serious to European troops.

Again, the knowledge of the country and the habits of the enemy (possessed in a remarkable degree by the Fantees) would be found of very great use, and could be turned to great account. Again, they would be less likely than the European soldiers to become the victims of an Ashantee surprise. Should Captain Glover succeed in his expedition, both as regards raising an army and leading it to success in the field, he will deserve the highest credit. It would be far more cheering to have better news of the state of affairs among the military men lately in service on the coast. Direct reform is needed, most of the officers having been engaged (to the prejudice of their proper work) as magistrates, secretaries, inspectors, &c. This is being remedied; and the arrival of Sir Garnet Wolseley at the seat of war has placed matters on a proper footing; but surely such maladministration ought not to have occurred to occupy any part of his valuable time. The state of affairs clearly explains the boldness of the Ashantees in attacking the British and Fantee settlements. The Ashantees were, no doubt, aware of the number of troops they would have against them, and of the small number of efficient officers to properly lead those troops. This evil seems to have been long in existence, and Colonel Harley did what he could with the small number of men at his disposal, and acted with much vigour and bravery, and thus saved worse disasters. The Ashantees were suddenly found at the very gates of the fort, and the evil glaringly shown up.

The British army is very small, therefore there is every need that it should be as efficient as experienced skill and foresight can make it. The news from the Gold Coast can travel but slowly, there being no telegraph; and we can but hope that Captain Glover is performing his hard task. Some considerable time will necessarily elapse before we can hear that he has taken offensive operations, and too much must not be expected on the arrival of the Commander in Chief; although it will be very satisfactory to learn his proposed mode of action, and what ultimate results he expects will follow. The last is, of course, the most important. It should not be considered that the soldiers are sent on a mere crusade against savages, nor is it necessary to seek fresh laurels in the shape of victories.

The work that is before them is definite, and to that it must be confined. The word of England is pledged to assist the Fantees and English residents on the coast and in the interior; and the army is sent for the purpose of making the British rule, and the British rule alone, felt by the Ashantees; to mete out punishment for past surprises and treachery, and take whatever means may be necessary to create a permanent Power, in order to guard against reprisals of any description.

When this is done it will then be time to determine what portion of the Ashantee Kingdom it is necessary to keep or protect, taking care to make clear our intentions to the natives.

We have no business to concern ourselves with the question of the civilization of West Africa. We are not waging any war with the bloody rites of the Ashantees, which are, no doubt, customs of a diabolical and brutal nature, long existing.

The repulse of the Ashantee invasion is what is required, and not the conversion of the Ashantee Kingdom. The miserable and barbarous customs of the Ashantees are as bad as they well can be, and no efforts of ours will permanently eradicate them. Nor should the Fantees and other friendly tribes be allowed to think that they can rely on our permanent assistance. The Fantees will doubtless again be established as a nation, as it is our policy to do so, and at the end of the war they will in all probability be left in possession of their own native army, that is, the army which Captain Glover purposes to form; and they must be given to understand that they must not expect future aid from British arms or future assistance in "border affrays."

It is certainly not the wish of the English people to be engaged in and to have to pay for perpetual hostilities. It is also very unfortunate that the only Power to which the actual duties are assigned is the British, although no doubt it is complimentary, and a tribute to us that we can use our power properly.

In fact, our past experience on the Gold Coast will have taught us that we must not consider ourselves invulnerable, therefore the more reason the authorities should guard against the ordinary fate of foreign powers making settlements of ever so small a nature.

We are probably working on safer ground than many countries or peoples have formerly occupied, and any foreign enmities we may awaken are not very likely to prove fatal to ultimate success.

The recent destruction of Chanah by a British man-of-war, for treachery, is not the first time Englishmen have assailed the town. According to Mr. Ferguson, it was destroyed in Queen Elizabeth's time by a person named William Towerson, described as a citizen of London as well as an adventurer of the Societies of Muscovia, Spain, and Portugal. This gentleman was a native of Cumberland. This description was given in the grant of arms made to him by Queen Elizabeth in acknowledgment of his voyages to Guinea, and for his destroying the towns of Chanah and Maura.

The Portuguese were the first discoverers of Guinea; they claimed the whole country, built many forts, and, among others, the fort of St. George, visited by Columbus, and now known by the name of Elmina. They endeavoured to, and did keep the whole of the trade to themselves for a long time, and they seized and confiscated all ships of other nations which tried to hold commerce with Guinea; the trade then consisted in gold, ivory, and pepper.

It appears that the first Englishman who traded with Guinea was one Thomas Windham, who sailed on his first voyage to that coast in 1551, and died during the third voyage, which took place in 1553: another Englishman, by name John Lok, succeeded him, and made a voyage in 1554.

COLONEL HARLEY

In the year 1555 William Towerson, before named, with the *Hart* and *Hinde* ships sailed for Guinea. He traded for gold, ivory, and pepper, and along the coast from the De Sestos River to Cape Three Points, and from there to Don John, a place near to the Castle of the Mine; from that fortress, the Portuguese made a sally, and, with the aid of the natives, attacked Towerson, but could not prevent him from trading with the residents on the coast. Towerson returned to England in April, 1556.

In the month of October, 1556, he again started, having under his control the *Tiger*, of 120 tons, the *Hart*, of 80 tons, and a pinnace of 16 tons.

On his arrival on the coast of Guinea, he found three French ships and two French pinnaces, with whom he allied himself. They traded along the coast as far as the Castle of the Mine, from whence five Portuguese ships came out to attack the allies. They manœuvred for two days, and Towerson's fleet got the weather gauge, and an action commenced. Towerson, in the *Tiger*, intended to board the Portuguese admiral, but after a few broadsides, Towerson had to retire, owing to the flight of the French ships, which, having afterward come up with, he treated to some shots. He then continued to trade along the coast, finally making off, pursued by the Portuguese ships. The *Hart* was wrecked on the voyage home, but the *Tiger*, after an action with a Frenchman, arrived in England in April, 1557.

Towerson made a third voyage. He then sailed with the *Minion*, the *Christopher*, the *Tiger*, and the *Unicorn* pinnace, from Plymouth, England and France being then at war; and the day after his start he captured two Dantsic ships laden with wine from Bordeaux; these he plundered. On his arrival at the Grand Canary he found there the Spanish West India fleet, of many sail. The admiral was barely civil; ordered Towerson to lower his flag, backing up his order by cannon shot. Towerson declined, cleared for action; demanded and obtained an apology. Towerson fought naval actions with both French and Portuguese, captured a French ship; and lastly, by a boat attack, plundered and burnt both Maura and Chanah, because the natives, by direction of the Portuguese, attacked his men. He either lost or had to abandon all his vessels but the *Minion*, which arrived in England a complete wreck, with but six merchants and six sailors on board in good health.

Towerson's voyages, as narrated by himself, are given in Hakluyl. As a reward for his exploits he received the grant of a crest—namely, a demi-Negro armed for the fight, and an addition to his coat of arms. A copy of this grant is in a valuable MS. heraldic visitation of Cumberland, in possession of Mr. Jackson, of Fleatham House, St. Bees. Between the second and third voyages of Towerson, Sir John Hawkins visited the coast of Guinea, and invented the slave trade. Sir John Hawkins on his return to England, in 1565, got an honourable addition to his arms, a demi-Moor bound with a cord, a crest still borne by his descendants.

In the year 1558 a company of London and Exeter merchants was formed to carry on the highly lucrative trade thus started by Windham, Lok, and Towerson.

It is clear that at the present time the Ashantees are supplied with fine foreign goods and ammunition to a large extent from the interior, and this clearly denotes want of free intercourse with the coast.

Major General Sir Garnet Wolseley, before starting for the Gold Coast, left orders that no filters of a complicated nature were to be sent for the use of the soldiers, but only those filters that could be readily cleaned. The best, no doubt, are the pocket filters, and these have been sent out. These little filters are simply a block of animal charcoal. Every soldier will be supplied with one.

In expectation of the rude kind of war in Ashantee, enormous quantities of gunpowder have been sent, as it is possible that rough work will have to be done;

indeed, in very recent wars, such as at Delhi, Magdala, and among the Maories of New Zealand, rude tactics have proved the best. Among civilized nations rockets are not much used in war, but in this war they will be found very effective. Hall's rockets in particular will be used. Materials for constructing a railway are being rapidly forwarded. Buckshot cartridges will be used, and some alteration has been made in their manufacture by the substitution of bone-dust for plaster of Paris, to fill in the interstices between the shots.

Very many officers have volunteered to join the Commander in Chief of the Expedition for service on the West Coast of Africa; in fact, more officers have volunteered than will be required for the expedition.

It is rumoured that the pumps used in the Abyssinian Expedition, as well as those returned from the Autumn Manœuvres, will be sent for the use of the army at Cape Coast. By providing suitable gear, these pumps can be worked by steam power supplied by the locomotives. The Government have been advised to send out English navvies to lay the railway, but they have determined that the work shall be done by the natives of the Gold Coast, who will work under the direction of the Royal Engineers.

The buckshot sent is manufactured by pressing and punching them out of sheets of lead, instead of casting the shot as formerly done. The cast shot was not always true. Lathes have been made for the purpose of making the shot: first rolling the metal into long rods; secondly, compressing these rods into bands, with bullets stamped upon them; thirdly, for punching out the bullets, which is the neatest part of the whole machinery; then rolling them between plates of steel until of the size required; and, lastly, polishing them and giving each a coating of black-lead. The star-shells, or night-lights, have been manufactured in very large quantities, and experiments have been made with these after dark, and they prove very successful.

A report has been current that all officers sent on service to the West Coast of Africa who possessed life assurance policies were compelled to forfeit them. This is not correct, although some Assurance offices have demanded extra premiums, which premiums will, however, guarantee the policy holders against all risks, either of foreign travel or any other contingencies.

CHAPTER IV.

Palinas—Imports—The Houssas—Major Hume—Kroomen—Sanitary conditions of Freetown—Ashantee camp—Coomassie—Produce of the country—Cost of the war—Wealth of King Koffee Calcalli.

PALINAS is the capital of Grand Canary. In the opinion of the residents of this town, the principal imports of America and Africa are yellow and other fevers; of European, cholera and other evils. The Grand Canary is a delightful winter resort. The island has a barren appearance, but it produces abundantly corn, wine, and cochineal. The inhabitants may be considered Spaniards of pure blood.

It is feasible that the original Carthaginians had large emporiums and factories for trade in these islands, and, without doubt, they possessed a colony in the sea beyond the Pillars of Hercules, and that in bad times they emigrated there, thus escaping from their enemies.

About the 14th century several mariners from Normandy, in the service of Castile, re-discovered the Canaries, which have ever since remained under the rule of Spain. The original natives, called the Guanches, were of Moorish race, who grew corn, and were quite ignorant of metal and its uses; they also preserved the bodies of the dead after the manner of the Egyptians.

Sir Garnet Wolseley, on his arrival at Cape Coast Castle, was sworn as governor. It is doubtful if any large force can be organised among the natives, except near the Gold Coast. The Fantees will prove extremely useful as an additional force only as, when brought face to face with the enemy, they will in all probability run away, and leave the unlucky officers to be killed. The Houssas are very good soldiers, but their numbers are small. Their native territory is in Central Africa. Operations will be commenced early in December, but the bush at all times is a mere lair of pestilence and consequent death.

The commercial aspects of the Gold Coast are extremely promising, but the results can never be known until we secure a lasting peace, and this will only be accomplished by vigorous action now, on the part of our Government and troops. Beyond doubt, the Ashantees invaded the territories under British protection in order to obtain easy access to the Gold Coast.* The rooted hatred to the Fantee tribe was no doubt the primary cause. When they do retire it will only be with the intention of returning.

What should be done is to secure for Englishmen and Fantees, and general allies, the same access over the country as the Ashantees at this time possess.

Major Hume, the principal of the engineering department, will have a large number of native carpenters and blacksmiths at work near the coast. The roads to be made will be constructed under his direction, and road making will be, for the first time, attempted in the Ashantee Kingdom. The principal obstacle the Commander in Chief will experience will be the enormous difficulty in procuring carriage. Lieut. Gordon of the 93rd Highlanders will also

---

* The Danish forts were acquired by purchase in 1851. The Dutch forts and territory in 1871.

raise native recruits near the coast. Two other officers will raise troops near the Gambia. Mr. O'Connor will endeavour to obtain Kroomen from Cape Palwas, who are admirable porters or carriers. Colonel Wood will be entrusted with the command of Elmina, and will also try to raise a native force, which, if he accomplishes, will earn him lasting credit, for he will have very inferior men to deal with. Sir Garnet Wolseley has obtained large powers from the Government, although he is still held down by unnecessary measures. The existing charter of the Gold Coast Government provides that in case of the death or absence of the governor, the Government shall be assumed by the gentleman who is acting at the time as collector of customs. However suitable such an arrangement may be in peaceful times, it seems very absurd for any collector or acting collector of customs to have control of military matters, and no directions have been given to alter the charter.

The streets in Freetown are bad, and call

for fresh sanitary measures, not only there, but in the existing British settlements. Dr. Robert Smith, the surgeon, who has the reputation of being a very attentive man, has made some valuable suggestions. He agrees with opinions expressed by Dr. Waters, and adds that, after long experience, he cannot remember the sanitary condition of Freetown worse than it is at present.

The good intentions of Lord Kimberley to improve the condition of the West African settlements will be quite useless, if he has not the means of obtaining more satisfactory information to guide him.

The following instance is a fair example of the very great evil and extreme inconvenience resulting from the system which prevails in Sierra Leone.

The distinguished Major Bravo, who has been for some time past in command of the 2nd West India Regiment, now on active service at Cape Coast, also holds the appointment of Police Magistrate of Freetown. The sum of £90 is allowed for six months' service for any person acting as a Police Magistrate. It frequently occurs that the gentleman who for this small sum undertakes to fulfil the last mentioned post, has many other duties to perform.

The power of the Police Court established at Freetown extends to a distance of *eight* miles outside the boundaries of the town. The sittings of the Court are held for the most part as early as six o'clock in the morning, and those of the inhabitants who reside at a distance, and who have to attend the Court at this untimely hour, have to get up as early as two or three o'clock in the morning. Moreover, when it is known how deadly in this climate is exposure to night air and dew, considerable surprise is expressed that additional dangers should be added to those already existing, and any rule more adapted to destroy the existing slight efficiency of the administration could not well be imagined.

Important posts are publicly sold. No European can live on this coast over eighteen months at a time and continue to be possessed of full mental and bodily powers. Consequently, periodical visits to England are required to restore his strength. Should he keep long on the coast, he withers away to an early death.

Roads should have been made years ago. Different systems of administration should prevail. Every officer, after eighteen months' or two years' REAL service, should be entitled to six months' leave of absence in England, and the Government should pay for or allow the expense. Officers should be encouraged to take regular leave, instead of having obstacles placed in their path. This is the only way to secure sound and useful administration, either in civil or military matters.

Even before the news had arrived at Cape Coast that Sir Garnet Wolseley had received the honour of acting as Commander in Chief, it was decided to attack the Ashantees in their camp at Mampon. This camp is seven miles from the British advanced redoubt, at a place called Abbah.

Captain Freemantle, the chief naval officer of the squadron, gallantly volunteered to garrison all the forts with blue jackets, so as to leave all the troops free for action. When, however, it was known that Sir Garnet was appointed, Colonel Feasting decided to defer any action until his chief arrived. Colonel Harley was, however, anxious to keep to the original programme, and attack at once; and Captain Freemantle expressed the same desire. The squadron are, at present, chiefly engaged in keeping up the blockade on the coast to the west of Elmina. Considerable sickness prevails at Cape Coast, and the heavy rains are still coming down.

Four trading brigs have been captured off the coast, and, on examination, proved to have a very large quantity of powder, &c., on board. Two of the ships proved to belong to an English firm, who, it is said, have made immense fortunes on the Gold Coast.

The working parties engaged in roadmaking will be always exposed to attacks from Ashantees, and every precaution should be used to prevent the gangs from being cut off.

Captain Glover speaks the native language, and hitherto he has been almost worshipped by the natives. He has only to appear and speak to them, when they will be excited to frenzy, and favour him with their wild dance and yells, and vow death to all Ashantees. This experienced and talented officer has capital materials for forming a splendid force, and, no doubt, he will use it well and rapidly.

The Ashantee capital must be entered, or held, or reduced to ashes, and the site occupied by the British, in order to dictate proper terms of peace.

Once the present Ashantee king, Koffee Calcalli, and his chiefs and people have been taught how useless it is to resist the great power of the British when such power is put forth, measures can easily be taken to secure a peace. Coomassie is not a fortress, and consequently of no value as a military position. No doubt, by the destruction of the town, many thousands of Ashantees will be reduced to famine and exposure; and if the capital can be occupied without destroying it, terms of peace of a durable character can be dictated from it, and this will be more consistent with the feelings of humanity. There are many towns in the interior much more populous than Coomassie, and, probably, to these the Ashantees will retire when it is destroyed. Any African town is easily destroyed; and, with the two exceptions of the king's palace and the Bantamnah at Coomassie, both of which are stone built, any town could be rebuilt as soon as the British retired.

A good road made to Coomassie will render the Ashantees powerless in future. Great neglect has been allowed, or roads would have been made before this. An enormous increase of trade may reasonably be expected when communication is thus made easy. Under past and present conditions free access is impossible. The

Ashantees have for many years desired free access with the coast.

It is an established fact that in the Ashantee Kingdom Gold and silver are found in large quantities, and numerous valuable plants grow freely. The country generally produces palm-oil, palm-kernels, and ground-nuts; sugar-cane, pepper, coffee, ginger, gum, and ivory are found in abundance; so that when once the interior is opened for English and European trade, a large demand will exist for English manufactured goods.

The expense of forming a railway will prove to be a highly remunerative investment, as it will open, for the purposes of trade, thousands of acres of hitherto useless country.

Probably the result of the expedition will happily prove to be the opening up of a vast and wealthy empire, available for successful commerce and missionary enterprise. The Ashantees are the only great tribe, and with them only is it necessary to treat to any considerable extent.

No difficulty will be experienced in making the Ashantees pay the cost of the war. A vast amount of treasure is stored at Coomassie, in the Bantamnah, and the Ashantees should be bound down to protect the railway and maintain the road, and they will soon understand that it is to their interest to keep faith with England. Whatever measures are decided upon should be carried out as early as possible, in the interests of commerce, humanity, and civilization. King Koffee Calcalli is fabulously rich, and at every Yam Custom hundreds of basinfuls of nuggets of gold are given to the king as presents. The hideous fever is the chief obstacle to progress. The natives will do any amount of work, provided they have good white overseers, and are well supplied with rum and money.

CHAPTER V.

The climate of the Gold Coast—Proper season for campaigning—The Netherlands expedition—Drink for the troops—Hospital accommodation—Extent of Ashantee Country and protected territory—Food and shelter—Quettah—Future of Africa.

ALTHOUGH the climate on the Gold Coast is generally very hot, it is considered more healthy than the climate of Sierra Leone. Very cold nights succeed hot days, and the general unhealthiness of the coast is caused by the varieties of temperature, and consequent miasma that rises, chiefly during the rainy season, from the swamps in the immediate neighbourhood of the streams and rivers. Although the interior of the country, so far as is known, is mostly covered with bush, it is more healthy; and the occupation of the higher lands has not proved very injurious to Europeans. Cholera and yellow fever have not yet been heard of, and, except in the very low districts near the coast, the climate is not so bad as is supposed. The soil is good, more especially around Axim.

It should be remembered that our best authorities seem agreed that the expedition should be undertaken and finished during the healthy months, and should not, in any case, be extended beyond March. The deadly sickness which befel our recently landed soldiers was probably due to their having been landed at the wrong time, and placed in lodgings in the unhealthy localities, indifferently supplied, perhaps, with the requisite diet, using bad water, and being subjected to great mental anxiety.

We have seen that the campaigns have always been undertaken at the wrong season, and the troops have not been supplied with proper food or pure water. Before Coomassie can be taken, the Ashantees will have to be dislodged from their present positions, which are now held in the unwholesome parts of the country. With the fall of the capital, and probable end of the war, ourselves and the neighbouring friendly tribes will be able to occupy more healthy permanent positions, without so much fear of molestation from the Ashantees.

It will be seen that it is quite possible, with care in choice of provisions and temperance on the part of the troops, to carry on and conclude this war without much more than the usual losses in such expeditions. When the expedition, in 1869, by the Government of the Netherlands to Kwassie Kron was carried out, no fever occurred in the army: their field flasks were kept well supplied with cold coffee, and spirits were strictly prohibited. And again, in 1864, some 400 sailors, &c., were landed from the *Rattlesnake*, and remained on shore for nearly two months, and this with a loss of only two men through fever. In this latter instance, also, no grog was allowed to be sold, and it seems that every attention was paid to the preservation of health. Of course, in all campaigns certain contingencies have to be provided for, change of climate among the rest; and with the experience of the past before the eyes of the authorities, everything for the health and comfort of the men should be readily provided. Great credit is due to the English doctors, there being plenty of medical volunteers, as in the case of the officers. No difficulty need therefore be experienced, for the medical men being fully aware of the dangers to health to be encountered by all, no pains have been spared in order to provide all necessary medical stores. No spirits will be allowed unless ordered by the doctors; and we believe the principal drink will be cold tea. Plenty of filtered water will be available for the use of the troops.

At night small fires should be used, both to guard against sudden changes in temperature and the miasma in the surrounding atmosphere.

Ample floating hospital accommodation should be provided, which will lessen the dangers arising from badly placed hospitals on land.

Every effort should be made to provide the troops, and especially the sick, with fresh meat and preserved vegetables. Ice is also considered by the medical profession as very essential for the proper treatment of the sick, and will be much needed in the climate near the coast.

In all probability no European soldiers will be required to remain on the Gold Coast during the rainy season; so that one of the principal sources of danger can be happily evaded.

The kingdom of the Ashantees, with the territories protected by the British, embraces an area of about 95,000 miles, and the country a perfect tableland of from 1,500 to 2,000 feet above the level of the sea, rising gradually to the base of the Kong Mountains. The Aquapim Hills, near Accra, rise to about 1,600 feet. The entire district, from about 45 miles north of the sea, may be described as one dense bush.

Rice is not grown on the Gold Coast, so that any quantity of that useful article will prove very acceptable to the troops. Mosquito nets should be provided; even the natives all along the coast are compelled to use them. The canvas tents generally used by soldiers would not be of any use in this climate, as they will not keep out a tropical rain, but they would keep in the torrid heat. The natives can anywhere construct a temporary shelter, by using palm leaves or long grass. Canvas water-coolers will be very useful; and, among other comforts to be provided, large quantities of citrate of magnesia have been ordered, and is the most refreshing drink that can be used.

During the fine season, that is, from November to April, and more especially in December, January, and February, the sea near the coast is very smooth; the temperature on board the ships is by no means disagreeable, there being plenty of refreshing breezes.

The town of Quettah is little more than fourteen hours' steaming from Cape Coast, and is near the entrance of the River Volta; so that a floating hospital would be of great use for any invalids, either from Captain Glover's force or from the troops under the command of Sir Garnet Wolseley.

Land hospitals should be erected on the Akropong Hills, in the main road or direction from Accra to Coomassie. On these healthy hills the Basle Mission has its home; and all the missionaries, their wives, and children, are healthy; so that the sick soldiers would have a blessing in the aid of these good people. This climate would prove of very great benefit to the fever-stricken. There are abundance of vegetables and fruits, and these hills are within easy distance of Volta and the neighbourhood of Coomassie. Galvanized wrought iron tanks, carbon cistern filters, and patent block charcoal filters, are to be supplied on board the ships, which will secure pure water being served out to the troops, for both cooking and drinking purposes. Perhaps there are some people who do not trouble themselves about the land of the jungle; but the day will probably come when Africa will occupy a good position among nations. The various descriptions given by men of note differ so much that no wonder Englishmen are incredulous, although the interest increases every day.

CHAPTER VI.

The priesthood—Their influence—Superstition of the natives—Doctors and soothsayers—Herbal knowledge —Unlucky days—Fetish—Occupations, &c.

IN most of the districts of the Ashantee Kingdom, in Cape Coast, Accra, and other portions of the territory, a priesthood takes the lead in religious matters. The priest acts as mediator between the people and the fetishes. The priests are also the protectors and have the management of the sanctuaries, if sanctuaries they can be called, and are also the teachers and executors of all statutes and laws ; they bear the reputation among the natives of being harmless, although it is the priests who order the dreadful rite of human victims, and who also delight in all the vicious oblations in the service of the fetishes. Many of the laws framed by these priests, referring to the protection of wells, to the dread of pigs, to the care to be exercised in the eating of yams before the yams are ripe, and to other sanitary acts, are merely used for the want of better authority to enforce the laws prevailing in the country.

There are two orders of priests. Those of the first order bear the title of " Soffoo," and priests of the second order claim the title of " Comfoo." In some parts there exists a third order, entitled "Accoomfooah," and this order includes all persons undergoing religious instruction.

Priests are regarded by the savages as immortal, and at a place known as Mananping, not far from Cape Coast, a large number of aged priests are considered to have lived in all time, and to have held immediate and constant communication with the fetish. To this spot the spirits of all old and good natives go, in order to become members in this world of ease and comfort with other holy spirits. A similar superstition is known to prevail among the North American Indians.

The dwellings used by the priests are small but convenient, and are similar to the circular houses still existing in some parts of the British Isles, and which are considered to have at one time formed part of the houses of the Druids.

The liberty and honours, as well as the property of the chief priests, are very great, and among the Fantee tribe the female priests are well versed in the properties of herbs, barks of trees, and the berries natural to the country. Some of these bear the name of "Doctor," and resemble, according to the accounts handed down to us, our Druids, although not particularly chaste.

Many offerings are made to the priests. Slaves sometimes give themselves to a priest, and can never be redeemed. A great impression as to the power of these priests exists, which debars the masters of slaves from redeeming their runaways; they believe that the entire destruction of all their relations would follow any attempt to recover their infatuated slaves or servants from the so-called "Church."

The name of "Comfoo" (the second order of priests) implies an order of medicine, and those bearing this title profess to be under the control of those bearing the first title, "Soffoo." They are, however, in fact, much more dangerous, more proud, and more secret in their operations, and are closely connected with the other orders. These doctors are the scholars, the soothsayers, the fortune-tellers, augurs, sorcerers, jugglers, and dealers in charms on the West Coast of Africa, and consequently keep the natives in the most rigorous subjection, compelling them to work to maintain them: they possess certain botanical knowledge, and are experts in curing the native sick, although they themselves appear to have but little faith in their method of doctoring the various prevalent diseases.

The Fantees believe that the "Comfoo" has every power over their health, their increase of families, the multiplication of their cattle, and over the duration of their lives. The mistake on the part of the natives consists in their having permitted themselves to rest satisfied in believing the power of the priests to be supernatural, whereas such power is certainly only derived by the astute "Doctors" from a general knowledge of the properties of the poisonous herbs, shrubs, and trees. Most of the tribes regard animals as their fetish. The Accras regard the hyena as their god; the residents in Anamaboo and neighbourhood revere the alligator; the Crobboes believe in the snake as their idol, and almost all the darkies adore the vulture.

The Ashantee kings have always given their devotions to white fowls, which, of course, they carefully protect. The rock on which the castle at Cape Town is built is called "Tharbirre," and is regarded by the Fantees as a fetish. Figures made of stone and wood, and supplied by the priests, are also believed to be fetishes. The Fantees observe a common fetish-day, which is on a Tuesday, when no work is done; the principal work of the Fantees on the coast is fishing, and this is never performed on a fetish-day. The last-named tribe also believe in lucky and unlucky days and months. September is considered by Fantees a lucky month for making their travels. Many of the Fantees have been as much as six weeks bringing a letter from the Ashantee King at Coomassie, but in September they accomplished their journey of about 180 miles in little more than a week.

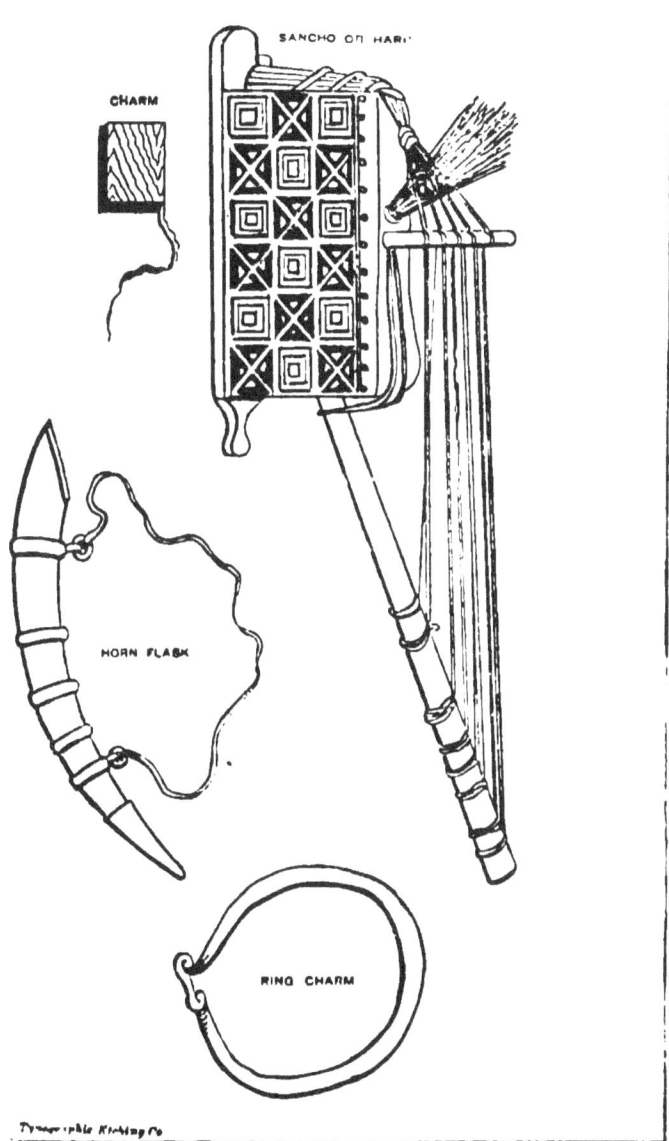

CHAPTER VII.

Arrival of [the Commander and Staff—Meeting of Native Kings—Speech of Sir Garnet Wolseley—King of Akim—Present State of Affairs.

THE vessel which carried Sir Garnet Wolseley and his staff arrived off Cape Coast Castle on the 2nd of October. Various rumours were afloat that our advanced post at Fort Napoleon, twelve miles from the Castle, could hear the beating of the native drums; that the Ashantees were planting corn, and intended to stay for three years; and that dysentery and smallpox were committing terrible ravages upon them. It was, however, officially believed that nothing certain whatever was known of the movements of the Ashantees, that they were equally ignorant of ours, and that these rumours were merely the tricks of the enemy's scouts or pretended deserters, who allowed themselves to be made prisoners. The proceedings which followed cannot be better described than in the language of the Special Correspondent of the *Standard* :—

"We lost no time in beginning the work of debarkation. As soon as the boats came alongside two officers went ashore to take charge of the baggage as it arrived, and the first boats took all our black labourers and servants. Then the work of landing the baggage began, and continued the whole day, for as in this country there is no meat and very little of anything else to be bought, every one had to bring a certain amount of stores, preserved provisions, wines, &c., in addition to his personal baggage; consequently the number of boxes and cases was very much above the amount which would, under ordinary conditions, be carried by forty officers. In addition to this there was the live stock brought down— thirty bullocks, sheep, &c. Lastly, there were no less than nineteen hundred packages belonging to the Engineers' department. The number of large boats available for the process of landing this cargo was but limited, and the distance to and from the shore considerable; consequently, when night fell it was found that little more than half the work was done. At half-past four Sir Garnet Wolseley landed. A small guard of honour was drawn up at the entrance to the castle, and the principal officers of the garrison were at the landing-place. Sir Garnet was accompanied by his staff, and by the rest of the officers, who will be for the present stationed here. The Elmina division was taken from the *Ambriz* direct to Elmina in the course of the morning by one of the steam launches of the fleet. Passing through the Castle, Sir Garnet proceeded through a double file, formed by soldiers of the 2nd West India Regiment, placed at intervals of ten paces, to the Government House. Here he was received by Colonel Harley, and by some of the chief functionaries of the place. The ceremony of swearing himself in here took place. The Supreme Judge assumed his wig, and Sir Garnet, laying his hand upon the Bible, took first the oath of allegiance, and then the oath as governor. In some respects, Sir Garnet's position differs materially from that of former governors. He is independent of Sierra Leone, and has full and absolute powers. The chief topic of conversation here, next to the landing of Sir G. Wolseley, is the great success which is attending the recruiting of Captain Glover. Men are flocking to him, and he has already five thousand of the seven thousand he intended to raise. It appears, however, that he is at present merely forestalling us, as he is recruiting at Accra, instead of up the Volta, as intended; and the men that he is taking are just those who would otherwise have naturally enlisted in the force which we have come to raise. There can be no doubt that Captain Glover is eminently qualified for his position as chief of an irregular body of natives. He has immense energy and great courage, and is looked up to with unbounded confidence by the natives.

"On October 4 a meeting took place, and the native kings have come face to face with the gentleman whom England has sent out to free them, if not for ever, at least for a generation or two, from the ever-present fear of their terrible enemies the Ashantees. The palaver was arranged to take place in two marquees, pitched together in the garden of the Government House, and immediately in front of the house. Government House is a structure of considerable size, built so as to give a free current of air across all the principal rooms, and in point of architecture a mere magnified copy of the merchants' houses around it. It stands in its own grounds, which have little to boast of in the way of gardening, but are brilliant with gorgeous coloured flowers, which abound everywhere. Its situation is badly chosen, as there is higher ground everywhere behind it; and had it been placed upon the hill a quarter of a mile in its rear, the lives of its occupants would have been worth considerably more than they are at present. The guard of honour in front of the house was furnished by the 2nd West India Regiment. The uniform is a very showy one, resembling closely that of a

Turco. The head-dress is a scarlet fez with a large pendant yellow tassel, a white turban enveloping the fez, which shows only on the top. The jacket is scarlet, with yellow braiding. The wide, loose pantaloons are black, and the gaiters are yellow. The kings began to arrive soon after three, and took their seats upon stools, carried for them by their attendants, at the farther end of the garden. They were in most cases preceded and announced by the beat of the tom-tom, while huge umbrellas were carried over their heads. The royal robes differed a good deal from each other, as some of the Cape Coast chiefs wore European attire. The others wore their robes in the Roman toga fashion, but the materials differed from plain printed calicoes to, in one case, scarlet velvet. With scarcely an exception, all had gold finger-rings, some of immense size, the gold projecting in knobs like walnuts. Some had massive and tastefully worked gold bracelets. One king wore a sort of crown or cap, composed apparently of a piece of a calabash or cocoanut, with strips of gold fastened into it. The stools of state differed as widely as their owners. One was a massive ebony arm-chair, with silver ornaments; others were of a plain, unvarnished, light-coloured wood, but elaborately carved. They were lightly made, probably for convenience of carriage. The seats were very wide, with a considerable bend downwards towards the centre. As the wood was thin and the legs far apart, it was evident that the weight of a man would try them severely. Each had, however, underneath the middle of the chair, a support in the shape of a fifth leg. It was not made of the same shape or size as the other legs, but was in the form of a cylinder of some four inches in diameter. This cylinder was perforated with holes, arranged in pattern, so that it was at once light and strong. Other stools were altogether unpretentious, and closely resembled a dairymaid's milking-stool. While four kings and a host of chiefs were gathering at the end of the garden a levee of officers and civilians was filling the vestibule and drawing-room of the Government House. Here were all the officers of the West India Regiments, in scarlet; all the officers of the fleet, in blue; and most of the officers of the expedition, in neat grey uniform. The staff, however, had for the most part brought out the full-dress uniform of the regiments to which they belong. Some of the Control and medical officers also came out in full dress. Among them were the civil staff of the colony and the leading merchants, white and coloured. Most of these were in black clothes, but others compromised with a black coat and light trousers, while one or two were entirely in white.

"Just at four o'clock, the appointed time, the Governor descended the steps to the marquee. The troops presented arms and the bugles sounded, and the sable monarchs advanced from their end of the garden. In a minute or two the tent was crowded, Sir Garnet Wolseley taking his stand upon a small raised dais at one end, with his officers behind him and along the side of the marquee, the interior of which was crowded with natives, who appeared to have no kind of respect for their kings, but pressed forward, each with an evident intention of seeing and hearing as much as he could. Remembering the meeting between Sir Robert Napier and King Cassa of Tigré, the followers of the latter were far more submissive in their behaviour than are these Fantees. Upon that occasion only King Cassa and his three nearest relatives and advisers were present, the rest staying outside the tent. The interview upon that occasion was, after the first greeting, carried on sitting, while here Sir Garnet Wolseley stood the whole time. One by one the kings and chiefs advanced, if the term advancing be applicable to the operation of violently squeezing one's way through a crowd. The interpreter named their titles, and Sir Garnet shook hands with each. After a time there was a pause, and then those who were known to be present, but whom either modesty or the crowd kept at a distance from the dais, were called forward. As a whole they were by no means a striking set of men; the only really notable one being the King of Abra, who stood six feet three inches high. He was not, however, of proportionate breadth, and stooped a good deal as he walked.

"This ceremonial lasted some time, from the number of those to be presented, and the time that it took some of them to get to the front. Most of the chiefs were preceded by gold-mace bearers, the maces being portentous in size, but, judging from the manner in which they were carried, very thin as to make. The presentations over, there was a long delay, as the bearers of the stools of the kings and chiefs pressed forward to place them for their lords while the address was being delivered. It was soon apparent that there was no room for all their stools, and the idea was at length abandoned; and although a few sat down, the greater portion of the kings and chiefs remained standing during its delivery. It was difficult to judge of their feelings by their faces.

"Sir Garnet Wolseley's speech was to the following effect:—

'I am very glad, so shortly after my arrival here, to meet so many kings and chiefs who are known to be loyal and faithful allies of Her Majesty. Her Majesty has learned with great concern the misfortunes which have befallen you, and the ravages which have been inflicted on your country. Being most anxious to assist you, she has sent me, conferring upon me supreme power, and uniting in my person the military and civil authority. I am desired to tell you that all measures which I may recommend after consultation with you on the subject will be carried out. It is, therefore, most essential that I should learn from you what you are prepared to do for yourselves. I can assure you that if you place all your available resources at my disposal I shall be prepared to guarantee to you that, with God's help, I shall inflict such a blow against Ashantee, that for all time you will be free from any dread of invasion. My desire is first to drive them out of your country, and I shall be prepared, if it be necessary, to follow them into their own country. It is, therefore, for you to consider to-day, amongst yourselves, as to what force each of you can place in the field to enable me to carry out my plan. Her Majesty will not help those who will not help themselves, and unless you are all prepared to do your best, and to make such sacrifices as you may be called upon to make, I tell you frankly that you must not look to the Queen for any assistance whatever. The line of forts which Her Majesty holds along the coast are so strong that they can bid defiance to any force whatever; and her only interest upon the coast is to enable you to enjoy the blessings of civilization, and to live in peace and happiness. In 1863-64 the Ashantees did not make war against the English, and this they took great pains to assert, their sole quarrel being with the Fantees; and it is in your interest only that we intervene in these disputes. Were Her Majesty to keep her troops within her forts, the practical result would be the entire destruction of the Fantees by the Ashantees. It is for you, therefore, to do your best for your own preservation. The terms which I am able to offer you are as follows:—To each chief I will give £10 per month for every thousand men he can raise. Large supplies of food are on their way from England, and I will, when they arrive, distribute a pound of rice and a quarter of a pound of salt meat to each fighting man per day. Until the supplies arrive I will give to each man the sum of $4\frac{1}{2}$d. per day instead of rations. I will also give to each fighting man 3d. per day pay. I will supply ammunition to the force, but I hope that you will be careful of it, and not repeat the lavish waste which I hear took place upon a late occasion. The supplies will be issued here at Cape Coast, and each king and chief must make arrangements for having them conveyed to his people wherever they may be, and this must be done without diminishing by one the number of fighting men. Each king and chief will be accompanied in the field by an English officer, who will convey my orders to you. Once in the field, there must be no flinching. If your people do not obey your orders, I will assist you to enforce my will upon them; but I must have throughout the most prompt and absolute obedience to my orders, for without this it is impossible that I can carry on the war successfully. Her Majesty has learned with pain that her allies have in some cases imitated the ferocity of their enemy by mutilating the dead and murdering prisoners. This must not be: any recurrence of this ferocious conduct will quite alienate the goodwill of those who most desire to help you. I am most anxious to know what you are each able to do. I hope, therefore, that you will consult this evening, and let me know at once what you can each do. Presents will be distributed this evening, as a token of the regard of Her Majesty, and of the pleasure which I have in now meeting you.

"This speech was translated sentence by sentence. At its end there was a pause, and it was thought that some of the kings or chiefs would speak. No one, however, evinced the slightest desire to do so, but one by one they approached Sir Garnet Wolseley, shook hands with him, and retired. Such was the end of the palaver; what its final result may be no one can yet say. The impression which the speech produced is, I hear, favourable, the only criticism which I have heard being that the offer of £10 per month to the chiefs for each thousand men they could raise and keep in the field was insufficient to induce those to exert themselves who would not do their best from a sense of patriotism without pay; but it is said on good authority that the power of these kings over their subjects is but small; they might order their tribe or village to take the field, but unless it perfectly suited their purpose, the people would refuse to go.

"The first step now to be taken is to find out where the Ashantees are, and with this object a detachment of the 2nd West India Regiment started to Donkora, twenty-five miles distant. Seven or eight of our officers have been out to survey the roads and country round. It has been determined to extend the blockade which now prevails on the Western Coast, or, as it is called here, the Windward Coast, to the Leeward ports, so as to prevent muskets and ammunition finding their way into the Ashantee Country. Two of the ports—Assimie and Grand Bassam—are French possessions; but the French have determined to co-operate with us, and will themselves declare a blockade of these ports.

"A week has now passed, and we have had two solemn palavers with black sovereigns. Sir Garnet Wolseley's energy has fairly communicated itself to the chiefs; and although it is by no means certain that they will be able to raise an army for us, it is now certain that they will endeavour to the utmost of their power to do so. Those who know them best are the most surprised to find that the kings are really keeping their word, and departing for their own countries. The greater portion of the officers who came out with us are leaving with these potentates, and will, by their presence, show the people that England is in earnest in their behalf.

"The following is the list of the officers as at present selected:—1. To King Eddoo of Mankesinu, Major Lazenby, 100th Regiment. 2. To King Ammono of

Annamaboe, Captain Godwin, 103rd Fusiliers. 3. To King Tehiboo of Assin, at Domonassie, Captain Bromhead, 24th Regiment. 4. To King Aquassie of Denkera, at Domonassie, Lieutenant Hearle, R.M.L.I. 5. To Chief Solomon Awoosse, of Domonassie, Sub Lieutenant Filleter, 2nd W.I. Regiment. 6. To King Amfoo Otto of Abrah, Lieutenant Pollard, R.N. 7. To King Assano of Yamolanza, Sub Lieutenant Lang, R.N. 8. To Quassie Aucama of Assiboo, Sub Lieutenant Corkran, R.N.

"The departure of some of these officers has, however, been delayed, owing to news which arrived from Captain Glover at Accra. The news goes to confirm what we have heard from other quarters. The intelligence is that the King of Ashantee, hearing that we are about to march upon Coomassie, has sworn the great oath to drive us altogether from his coasts; that he has collected every fighting man in his kingdom, and is already seventeen days on his march towards Cape Coast. This town is strong now; in a few days it will be impregnable to an undisciplined enemy. In addition to Forts William and Victoria, a chain of redoubts have been thrown up during the last few days upon the other heights, which form a circle round the town. These are now ready to receive their guns, and, manned by seamen or marine artillerymen, will give the Ashantees such a reception that they will never again care about meeting the terrible arms of the white man.

"Attah, King of Akim, whose territories lie slightly to the west of north of Accra, and extend to the border of Ashantee, has joined us heart and soul. The Akims were formerly vassals of the Ashantees, but some time since regained their independence. The other day four messengers arrived to Attah from the King of Ashantee with the salutation, 'The King, our master, sends us to say that he has no palaver with you, only with the Fantees. He wishes you to have nothing to do with this quarrel.' Attah took a night to refleet, and in the morning summoned the four messengers to his presence. Heralds are not, unfortunately for themselves, sacred personages in Africa. The King accordingly struck off the heads of two of the messengers, sent another back to the King of Ashantee with the news that the King of Akim would fight him to the death, and himself brought the fourth messenger down to Captain Glover at Accra. Here Attah swore a great oath on his sword to Captain Glover that he would aid him with his whole force, and that he would accompany him wherever he went. As the King of Akim can put 20,000 fighting men in the field this is an alliance which will be of the greatest utility to us. He told Captain Glover that he wanted no money, only guns and ammunition. The King of Denkera promised at the late palaver to raise his tribe. Accra has already joined us, and with these three powers we shall, no doubt, have the Assins. These four tribes can, between them, turn out an army fully equal to that of Ashantee, and it is only their mutual jealousies which have enabled the Ashantees to tyrannise over the whole coast.

"Of them all, Akim is the most warlike, and this frank adhesion of its king will immensely strengthen our hands. It shows, at any rate, that the tribes who have hitherto been too often encouraged to fight the Ashantees, and then left in the lurch by the English authorities, have faith in the news that has been spread among them that this time England is in earnest, and really intends to strike a blow herself at the common foe. The work of roadmaking is progressing. There is now a fair road —that is, a fair road for this country— finished to Dunqua, and Gordon is at work on it beyond.

"One word more on the climate of Cape Coast Castle. Almost anything will grow with the smallest attention. Oranges, bananas, palms, custard apples, limes, and pine-apples are indigenous; the sugar-cane and tobacco would flourish; even European products — lettuces ,radishes, &c. — are grown with great success by some of the English merchants in their gardens; and yet the jungle extends, almost untouched by the hand of man, right up to the town. It cannot be doubted that the clearance of this rank vegetation, and the substitution of cultivated ground, would greatly decrease the miasma in the wet season, and would in equal proportion improve the health of the town. The Cape Coast negroes are far less advanced in civilization and deterioration than are the Sierra Leone men; but they have already sunk below all the other tribes near the coast. They are faithless and cowardly, and are become a byword among the other tribes. It is probable that with another half-century of civilizing they will sink physically and intellectually to the level of the Sierra Leone negro."

A

CATALOGUE OF BOOKS

PUBLISHED BY

JAMES BLACKWOOD & CO.

LONDON:
8, LOVELL'S COURT, PATERNOSTER ROW.

James Blackwood & Co., Publishers,

BLACKWOOD'S
Universal Library of Standard Authors.

In royal 8vo, cloth, Illustrated, 5s. each.

1. THE LIFE OF DR. SAMUEL JOHNSON, with his Correspondence and Conversations. By JAMES BOSWELL, Esq. Edited, with copious Notes and Biographical Illustrations, by EDWARD MALONE. Unabridged edition. Illustrated.

2. THE COMPLETE WORKS OF OLIVER GOLDSMITH. Comprising his Letters, Essays, Plays, and Poems. With a Memoir by Professor SPALDING, and a fac-simile of a characteristic and humorous Letter of Goldsmith to a Friend, and other Illustrations.

3. THE COMPLETE WORKS OF ROBERT BURNS AND SIR WALTER SCOTT, with Portraits and a fac-simile of a Sonnet, and a characteristic Letter of Burns to Mr. Riddell, and other Illustrations.

4. THE COMPLETE POETICAL WORKS OF MILTON AND YOUNG, with Portrait and Illustrations.

5. THE COMPLETE POETICAL WORKS OF GRAY, BEATTIE, BLAIR, COLLINS, THOMSON, AND KIRKE WHITE, with a fac-simile of the MS. of Gray's Elegy, and other Illustrations.

6. MASTERPIECES OF FICTION. By Eminent Authors, comprising Knickerbocker's New York, by WASHINGTON IRVING; The Linwoods, by Miss SEDGWICK; Elizabeth; or, The Exiles of Siberia; Paul and Virginia; The Indian Cottage; and Rasselas, by Dr. JOHNSON. With Portrait of Washington Irving, and other Illustrations.

7. MASTERPIECES OF FOREIGN LITERATURE, comprising Schiller's Tragedies, Goethe's Faust: Translated from the German by COLERIDGE and FILMORE; La Fontaine's Fables, and Saintine's Picciola; or, The Prison Flower. Unabridged, with Portrait and other Illustrations.

8. ROBINSON CRUSOE, OF YORK, MARINER; with an Account of his Travels round Three Parts of the Globe, with Eight Illustrations by Zwecker, engraved by Dalziel, and Eight Steel Illustrations by Stothard, engraved by Charles Heath.

9. ANECDOTES, LITERARY AND SCIENTIFIC, illustrative of the Characters, Habits, and Conversation of Men of Letters and Science. Edited by WILLIAM KEDDIE. Illustrated.

10. THE ARABIAN NIGHTS' ENTERTAINMENTS. Translated from the Arabic. New edition, with 100 Illustrations.

Series to be continued.

8, Lovell's Court, Paternoster Row, London.

Five-Shilling Series.

Elegantly bound in cloth, and Illustrated, small post 8vo, 5s. cloth.

1. **YOUNG BENJAMIN FRANKLIN**: Showing the Principles which raised a Printer's Boy to First Ambassador of the American Republic. By HENRY MAYHEW. 8 Illustrations by John Gilbert.

2. **ROMANCE AND REALITY.** By L. E. L., with a full Memoir and Portrait of the Author, and other Illustrations.

    "Thus have I begun:
    And 'tis my hope to end successfully."

3. **THE ROYAL HOLIDAY AND YOUNG STUDENT'S BOOK**: Being the "Holiday Book for the Young" and the "Young Student's Holiday Book" complete in One Volume. Numerous Illustrations.

4. **INDOOR AND OUTDOOR GAMES FOR ALL SEASONS**: Being Parlour Pastimes and Games for all Seasons. Complete in One Volume. Numerous Illustrations.

5. **STORIES OF THE CONQUESTS OF MEXICO AND PERU**, with a Sketch of the Adventures of the Spaniards in the New World, retold for Youth. By WILLIAM DALTON. With 8 Illustrations by Gilbert.

6. **THE POWDER MONKEY**; or, The Adventures of Two Boy Heroes in the Island of Madagascar. By WILLIAM DALTON.

7. **THE WESTERN MARTYROLOGY**; or, Bloody Assizes: containing the Lives, Trials, and Dying Speeches of all those eminent Protestants that suffered in the West of England and elsewhere from the year 1678; together with the Life and Death of Judge Jeffreys.

8, Lovell's Court, Paternoster Row, London.

Blackwood's Edition of the Poets

Large fcap. 8vo, Illustrated, 3s. 6d. cloth extra, gilt edges.

1. CHOICE SELECTIONS FROM THE BRITISH POETS, from Spenser to Robert Montgomery. Eight Illustrations.
2. POETICAL WORKS OF H. W. LONGFELLOW. Eight Illustrations. From the last American edition.
3. POETICAL WORKS OF ALEXANDER POPE, with a Memoir of the Author, Notes and Critical Notices of each Poem. By the Rev. Dr. CROLY. With Portrait and other Illustrations.
4. THE POETICAL WORKS OF ROBERT BURNS, with Memoir complete. Portrait and other Illustrations.
5. THE POETICAL WORKS OF JOHN MILTON. Complete, with Channing's Essay. Portrait and other Illustrations on Steel.
6. THE POETICAL WORKS OF SIR WALTER SCOTT, with Life of the Author. Portrait and other Illustrations on Steel.
7. LAMB'S TALES FROM SHAKESPERE. By CHARLES and MARY LAMB. With Scenes illustrating each Tale. Edited by CHARLES KNIGHT. 16 Illustrations.
8. THE POETICAL WORKS OF WILLIAM COWPER. With an Introductory Essay by JAMES MONTGOMERY. Eight Illustrations.
9. THE POETICAL WORKS OF HENRY KIRKE WHITE. Eight Illustrations.
10. THE POETICAL WORKS OF THE REV. GEORGE CRABBE. Eight Illustrations.
11. THE POETICAL WORKS OF THOMAS MOORE, with Memoir, Explanatory Notes, &c. Eight Illustrations.
12. THE POETICAL WORKS OF WORDSWORTH, with Memoir, Explanatory Notes, &c. Eight Illustrations.
13. THE POETICAL WORKS OF LORD BYRON, with Explanatory Notes, &c. Eight Illustrations.

8, Lovell's Court, Paternoster Row, London.

CHOICE READING.

Books suitable for Presents, Libraries, &c.

Large fcap. 8vo, Illustrated, extra cloth, 3s. 6d., gilt edges and side.

1. **MEN WHO HAVE MADE THEMSELVES**: Whence they Started; How they Journeyed; What they Reached. A Book for Boys. Numerous Illustrations and Portraits. 15th thousand.

This Work is issued with the view of exciting in the young a spirit of noble emulation, and a desire for true greatness. The Lives of upwards of Thirty Men who have distinguished themselves in Science, Commerce, Literature, and Travel, are told with spirit. It will be found the best book of the kind ever issued.

Contents.—HUMPHRY DAVY, the Inventor of the Spirit Lamp—JAMES FERGUSON, the Shepherd-boy Astronomer—JAMES WATT, the Inventor of the Steam Engine—GEORGE STEPHENSON, the Inventor of the Locomotive Engine—GIOVANNI BATTISTA BELZONI, the Traveller in Egypt—WILLIAM CAXTON, the First English Printer—JAMES COOK, the Discoverer of South Sea Islands—BENJAMIN WEST, the Quaker Artist—SIR WILLIAM JONES, the Oriental Scholar and Jurist—SIR HENRY HAVELOCK, the Christian Soldier—JOHN LEYDEN, the Poet and Asiatic Scholar—WILLIAM GIFFORD, the Learned Shoemaker—ALEXANDER WILSON, the Ornithologist of America—ROBERT BLOOMFIELD, the Poet of the Farm—ROBERT BURNS, the Poet of the World—COUNT RUMFORD, the Chemist of Comfort—JOHN WYCLIFFE, the First Protestant—GEORGE BUCHANAN, the Tutor of an English King—THOMAS RUDDIMAN, the Grammarian—ALEXANDER ADAM, the High School Rector—BARON HUMBOLDT, the South American Traveller JOHN SMEATON, the Builder of the Eddystone Lighthouse—ROBERT PEEL, the Spinner—JAMES MORRISON, the Warehouseman—BENJAMIN FRANKLIN, the Wise Printer—WILLIAM COBBETT, the Plough-boy Politician—PETER HORBERG, the Peasant Artist—HUGH MILLER, the Geologist Stonemason—ELI WHITNEY, the Inventor of the Cotton Gin—RICHARD ARKWRIGHT, the Inventor of the Cotton Water Frame—JOHN OPIE, the Carpenter Artist—SAMUEL BUDGETT, the Conscientious Grocer—THOMAS SCOTT, the Commentator on the Bible—RICHARD BAXTER, the Fervent Preacher—LOTT CARY, the Negro Colonist—WILLIAM EDWARDS, the Persevering Bridge Builder—R. STEPHENSON, the Railway Engineer.

2. **THE LION OF WAR**; or the Pirates of Loo Chow. A Tale of the Chinese Seas, for Youth. By F. C. ARMSTRONG, Esq. Eight Illustrations.

   This is a book of Adventures and Incidents for Boys.

3. **LUCY NEVILLE AND HER SCHOOLFELLOWS.** A Book for Girls. By MARY and ELIZABETH KIRBY. Eight Illustrations. Fourth Thousand.

   "Do justice, love mercy, and walk humbly with thy God."

5. **THE LIFE AND TRAVELS OF ALEXANDER VON HUMBOLDT** : with an Account of his Discoveries, and Notices of his Scientific Fellow-Labourers and Contemporaries. Eight Illustrations.

Contents.—Early Life—The Voyage and Visit to the Canary Islands—Excursions about Cumana — Towards the Orinoco—Up the Orinoco—To Cuba and Back—Colombia and Peru—Mexico—Results of Humboldt's Travels — Journey to Central Asia—Last Literary Labours.

6. **THE MILITARY HEROES OF ENGLAND**, from the Invasion of Julius Cæsar to the Present Time. Eight Illustrations. Tenth Thousand.

Contents.—The Ancient Britons and their Roman Conquerors—Saxon and Danish Rule—William of Normandy—Richard the Lion Hearted—Reigns of John and Henry III.—Edward I., and his Wars with the Welsh and Scots—Edwards II. and III.—Wars with Scotland, Wales, and France—The Wars of the Roses—The Tudor Sovereigns—Cromwell—William of Orange—Marlborough—Jacobite Rebellions—Chatham, Wolfe, Clive—War with United States, India, &c.—Wellington, Moore—Wars with Affghans, Sikhs. Sir C. Napier—Crimea, Indian Mutiny, Havelock, Sir C. Campbell, &c., &c.

10. **A POPULAR BOOK ON FLOWERS, GRASSES AND SHRUBS.** With Anecdotes and Poetical Illustrations ; a Glossary of Botanical Terms, and a Copious Index. By MARY PIRIE. Numerous Illustrations.

A most excellent Book for Young Ladies.

11. **ILLUSTRIOUS MEN** : Their Noble Deeds, Discoveries, and Attainments. Tenth Thousand. Eight Illustrations.

Contents.—Alfred the Great — Geoffrey Chaucer — Cardinal Wolsey—Sir Thomas More—Thomas Cromwell, Earl of Essex—Hugh Latimer, Bishop of Worcester—John Jewell, Bishop of Salisbury—Sir Thomas Gresham—The Admirable Crichton—Sir Francis Drake—William Cecil, Lord Burleigh—William Shakespere—Sir Walter Raleigh — Francis Bacon — Sir Edward Coke —Thomas Wentworth, Earl of Strafford—John Hampden—Dr. William Harvey—Admiral Blake—Edward Hyde, Earl of Clarendon—John Milton—John Tillotson—John Locke—Gilbert Burnet, Bishop of Salisbury—William Penn—Joseph Addison—John Churchill, Duke of Marlborough—Sir Isaac Newton—Robert Walpole—John Dalrymple, Earl of Stair—Sir Hans Sloane—General Wolfe—George, Lord Anson — George, Lord Lyttelton — William Pitt, Earl of Chatham—Sir William Blackstone—Dr. Samuel Johnson—Robert Lowth, Bishop of London—John Howard—William Murray, Earl of Mansfield.

James Blackwood & Co., Publishers,

12. ILLUSTRIOUS WOMEN who have Distinguished Themselves for Virtue, Piety, and Benevolence. 8 Illustrations.

Contents.—Queen Victoria—Princess Frederick William of Prussia, the Princess Royal—The Empress Eugenie—the Duchess of Kent—Queen Adelaide—Lady Jane Grey—Mary, Queen of Scots—Queen Caroline—Queen Marie Antoinette—Josephine, Queen and Empress—Lady Rachel Russell—Elizabeth Fry, the Prison Reformer—Harriet Martineau—Amelia Opie—Lady Huntingdon—Hannah More—Eliza Cook—Felicia Hemans—Mrs. Bunyan—Charlotte Corday—Frederika Bremer—L. E. L.—Jenny Lind—Joan of Arc—Miss Coutts—Florence Nightingale—Elizabeth, Anna, and Emily Blackwell.

13. MERCANTILE MORALS. A Book for Young Men entering upon the Duties of Active Life. With an Appendix, containing a popular Explanation of the principal Terms used in Law and Commerce, with the Moneys, Weights, and Measures of Foreign Countries, and their English Equivalents. Tenth Thousand.

Contents.—Wealth not the Chief End of Life—Mercantile Morality—Making Haste to be Rich—Dangers incident to Young Men in Large Cities—The Young Merchant needs a Guide—The Young Merchant in Society—Unsuccessful Merchandise, or, Sabbath Desecration—Forbidden Gains—The Young Merchant opposes the Bible—The Young Merchant a Novel Reader—The Young Man at the Theatre—Sketch of the History of English Trade and Commerce—Principal Terms used in Trade and Commerce, &c., &c.

14. THE REMARKABLE SCENES OF THE BIBLE ; or, The Places distinguished by Memorable Events recorded in Scripture. By the late Rev. Dr. HUGHES, Rector of St. John's, London. Numerous Illustrations.

Contents.—Eden—Ararat—Babel—Ur, Haran, Moreh—Sodom and Gomorrah—Moriah—Bethel—Shechem—Dan and Beersheba Egypt—The Red Sea—The Wilderness—Rephidim—Sinai—Hor and Pisgah—Jordan—Gilgal—Jericho—Gibbon—Shiloh—Ramoth Gilead—Carmel—Bethlehem.

15. LECTURES ON THE PARABLES OF OUR SAVIOUR. By Rev. Dr. KIRK. With Preface by Professor MCCRIE.

16. THE RELIGION OF GEOLOGY AND ITS CONNECTED SCIENCES. By EDWARD HITCHCOCK, D.D., LL.D. With Corrections and an Additional Lecture, giving a Summary of the Author's Present Views on the whole subject, and a copious Index. Extra cloth. (Cheap Edition, 2s.)

Contents :—Revelation Illustrated by Science—The Epoch of the Earth's Creation Unrevealed—Death a Universal Law of Organic Beings on this Globe from the Beginning—The Noachian Deluge Compared with the Geological Deluges—The World's supposed Eternity—Geological Proofs of the Divine Benevolence—Divine Benevolence as Exhibited in a Fallen World—Unity of the Divine Plan and Operation in all Ages of the World's History—The Hypothesis of Creation by Law—Special and Miraculous Providence—

8, Lovell's Court, Paternoster Row, London.

The Future Condition and Destiny of the Earth—The Telegraphic System of the Universe—The Vast Plans of Jehovah—Scientific Truth, Rightly Applied, is Religious Truth—Synoptical View of the Bearings of Geology upon Religion.

17. DOGS: Their Sagacity, Instinct, and Uses, with Descriptions of their several Varieties. By GEORGE FREDERICK PARDON. Illustrated by HARRISON WEIR.

18. THE HOLIDAY BOOK FOR THE YOUNG: Being Short Readings in History, Geography, Natural History, Theology, Physics, &c. By WILLIAM MARTIN. With numerous Illustrations. Seventh Edition.

"A work to amuse and instruct, to enlighten the mind and purify the affections."

Contents:—Ancient History — Bible Lessons — Boat-Building—Butterflies—Different Kinds of Ships—History, Geography, and Chronology—History of Ancient Egypt—Lessons on the Lord's Prayer—My Grandfather's Stories—Natural History—Natural Theology—Physics—Picture Lessons—Poetry — Flowers — Teachings from Nature — Thanksgiving for Existence — The Birds — The Flowers—The Juvenile Lecturer—The Life, Travels, and Adventures of Reuben Ramble—The Moon—The Selfish Boy—The Stars—The Sun—The Wonders of Geology.

19. THE YOUNG STUDENT'S HOLIDAY BOOK: Being Lessons on Architecture, Mechanics, Natural History, Manufacture of Pottery, &c. By WILLIAM MARTIN. Seventh Edition. With numerous Illustrations.

Contents—A Chronological Epitome of the History of Architecture in England—Austrian Salt Mines—A Wild Boar Hunt—Bible Lessons—Cleanliness—Coal and Gas—Evening Prayer—History of Macedon—Persia—Lessons on Things—Lessons on the Lord's Prayer—Mechanics—Morning Prayer—My Grandfather's Stories—Natural History—Physics—Picture Lessons—Architecture—Poetry—Steam and the Steam-engine—Teachings from Nature—The Electric Telegraph—The Juvenile Lecturer: Earthenware and Porcelain—Ancient Pottery—Porcelain Manufacture—Preparation of Clay and Flints—Manufacture of Pottery—Painting, Gilding, &c.—The Pump—The Stereoscope.

20. STORY OF THE PENINSULAR WAR. By the late MARQUIS of LONDONDERRY, Colonel of the Second Regiment of Life-Guards. With continuation by G. R. GLEIG. With Portraits and Illustrations. This work contains a lucid description of the momentous period between 1789 and 1815. All the Battles are described and notices of the leading Generals inserted.

21. LIFE AND ADVENTURES OF DR. LIVINGSTONE IN THE INTERIOR OF SOUTH AFRICA; comprising a Description of the Regions which he traversed, an Account of Missionary Pioneers, and Chapters on Cotton Cultivation, Slavery, Wild Animals, &c., &c. By H. G. ADAMS. With Portrait and Numerous Illustrations.

8, Lovell's Court, Paternoster Row, London.

Contents—The Boy, the Man, the Missionary—Missionary Pioneers—Mamaqualand and the Griguas—Among the Bechuanis—Lake Ngami—To St. Paul de Loanda—Back to Linyanti—Visit to Moselekatse—Away to Quillimane—Wild Animals of South Africa—Cotton Cultivation and Slavery—Journey Home—Recent Information.

22. **THE EARTH**: Its Physical Condition, and most Remarkable Phenomena. By W. M. HIGGINS. Sixth Edition. Numerous Illustrations.

Contents—The Earth in Relation to the Universe—Celestial Appearances—The Atmosphere and its Properties—Atmospherical Phenomena Dependent on the Distribution of Heat—Light—Electricity—Terrestrial Magnetism—Interior of the Earth—Land and Water—Superficial Temperature of the Earth.

23. **HALF-HOURS WITH OUR SACRED POETS.** Edited, with Biographical Sketches, by ALEXANDER H. GRANT, M.A. 8 Illustrations. Nearly Two Hundred select Pieces from the writings of more than Eighty Authors of Sacred Poetry are embraced in this volume, from the Fourteenth Century to the Present Time.

24. **CURIOSITIES OF PHYSICAL GEOGRAPHY**, comprising Avalanches, Icebergs, Trade Winds, Earthquakes, Volcanoes, also Reflections on the Connexion between the Physical Condition of a Country and the Mental Development of its Inhabitants, &c. By W. WITTICH. 8 Illustrations.

Contents — Snow-Mountains — Glaciers—Avalanches—Mountain-slips—Icebergs and Ice-fields—The Gulf Stream—The Simoom—Trade-Winds—Monsoons—Plains and Deserts—The Sahara—The Selva, or Forest Desert of the Amasonas—The Pampas—The Llanos—Earthquakes—Volcanoes.

25. **POPULAR NATURAL HISTORY AND CHARACTERISTICS OF ANIMALS**, with Illustrative Anecdotes. By Capt. T. BROWN.

Contents—Anecdotes of Animals—The Horse Kind—The Cow Kind—The Sheep Kind—The Deer Kind—The Hog Kind—Of the Cat Kind—The Dog Kind—The Weasel Kind—The Hare Kind—The Rat Kind, &c.—The Bat Kind.

26. **HABITS AND CHARACTERISTICS OF ANIMALS AND BIRDS**, with numerous Anecdotes. By Capt. T. BROWN.

Contents—Amphibious Animals—Of the Monkey Kind—The Monkey Proper—Of Pouched Animals, The Great Kangaroo—Of the Elephant—Rhinoceros—Hippopotamus—Cameleopard or Giraffe—Camel and Dromedary—Bear—Badger—Racoon—Anecdotes of Birds, Ostrich, Emu, Cassowary, Dodo, Solitaire—Of Rapacious Birds, Eagle, Condor of America, Vulture, Falcon, Jer-Falcon, Common Falcon, Kestrel, Hobby, Merlin, Goshawk, Sparrow Hawk, Kite, Buzzard, Butcher Bird—The Owl Kind, Horned or Eagle Owl, Common Horned Owl, Long-eared Owl, Snowy Owl,

8, Lovell's Court, Paternoster Row, London.

Barn Owl, Tawny Owl—Of Birds of the Poultry Kind, The Cock Peacock, Turkey, Pheasant, Guinea Hen, Bustard, The Grouse and Its Congeners—The Partridge and Its Varieties—Birds of the Pie Kind—The Magpie and its Congeners—Jay—The Woodpecker and its Congeners, Wryneck, Nuthatch—The Cuckoo and its Varieties—The Parrot and its Congeners—The Pigeon and its Congeners, Rock Dove, Ring Dove—Birds of the Sparrow Kind, Song Thrush, Missel Thrush, Blackbird, Redwing, Fieldfare, Ring Ouzel, Water Ouzel, Starling, Sparrow, Greenfinch, Crossbill, Grossbeak, Chaffinch, Yellow Hammer, Bunting, Siskin, Wheatear—The Nightingale and other Soft-billed Birds, Nightingale, Redbreast, Sky-Lark, Wood-Lark, Grasshopper-Lark, Black-cap, Blue Titmouse, Wren, House Wren, Golden Crested Wren, Willow Wren, Wood Wren—White-ear—Pied Wagtail, Grey Wagtail, Yellow Wagtail—Rock or Shore Pipit—Meadow Pipit or Tit—The Canary and other Hard-billed Song Birds—Goldfinch—Bullfinch—Common or Brown Linnet—Mountain Finch or Brambling—The Swallow and its Congeners—House Swallow—Chimney Swallow—Swift—Cape Swallow—Sand Martin—Cliff Swallow—Esculent Swallow—European Goat-sucker—The Humming Bird and Its Varieties.

27. **ILLUSTRATIVE ANECDOTES OF BIRDS, FISHES, AND INSECTS, &c.** By Captain T. BROWN.

Birds of the Crane Kind—Small Birds of the Crane Kind—Water-Fowl—The Penguin Kind—Birds of the Goose Kind—The Duck and its Varieties—Cetaceous Animals—Fishes in General—The Shark Tribe—The Ray Tribe in General—The Lamprey and its Congeners—Sturgeons in General—Spinous Fishes—The Mackerel Tribe—The Chætodon Tribe—The Perch Tribe—Surmullets in General—Gurnards in General—The Doree Tribe—Sticklebacks—The Mullet Genus—Eels in General—The Cod Tribe—Flat Fish in General—The Sucking Fish Tribe—The Salmon and its Congeners—The Pike and its Congeners—The Herring and its Congeners—Flying Fish in General—The Carp and its Congeners—Crustaceous Animals in General—The Tortoise and its Congeners—Testaceous Shell Fish—The Frog Tribe—Lizards and their Congeners—Serpents in General—Anecdotes of Insects—Concluding Remarks on Insects—Worms—Zoophytes—Animalculæ.

28. **THE PILGRIM'S PROGRESS FROM THIS WORLD TO THAT WHICH IS TO COME**, delivered under the similitude of a dream, wherein is discovered the manner of his setting out, his dangerous journey, and his safe arrival at the desired country. In three parts. By JOHN BUNYAN. "I have used similitudes"—*Hosea* xii. 10. With Eight Page Illustrations.

29. **LIVES OF THE BRITISH ADMIRALS AND NAVAL HISTORY OF GREAT BRITAIN**, from the Days of Cæsar to the Present Time. By Dr. JOHN CAMPBELL. Seventh Edition. Revised and Corrected. Illustrated by Portraits Numerous Facsimiles and Engravings, and Plans of Battles.

Contents—CHAPTER I.—The Britons—The Romans—The Saxons—The Danes—The Normans—Alfred—Cœur-de-Lion—Reign of

Henry the Seventh—Origin of the Royal Navy as a distinct service
—Henry the Eighth—Edward the Sixth—Mary—Sir John Cabot—
Sebastian Cabot—Howard—Sir John Dudley.

CHAPTER II.—Reign of Elizabeth—Her precautions to restore
her Fleet—The Spanish Armada—Howard of Effingham—Earl of
Essex—Sir John Hawkins—Sir Francis Drake—Sir Martin Frobisher
—Earl of Cumberland—Sir Robert Dudley—Sir Richard Grenville—
James Lancaster.

CHAPTER III.—Reign of James the First—Sir William Monson—
Quarrels with the Dutch—Sir Walter Raleigh—Reign of Charles the
First—Sir Robert Mansel—Sir William Monson.

CHAPTER IV.—Naval History during the Commonwealth—The
Protectorate—Wars with the Dutch—War with Spain—Admiral
Blake—The Restoration—Charles II.—Struggle with the Dutch for
the Sovereignty of the Seas—James II.—Duke of Albermarle—Earl
of Sandwich — Prince Rupert — Lawson — Kempthorne—Ayscue—
Spragge.

CHAPTER V.—Reign of William and Mary—War with France—
Reign of Anne, 1689 to 1714—War with France and Spain—
Admiral Benbow—Sir Cloudesley Shovel—Sir George Rooke, and
others.

CHAPTER VI.—Reign of George I., 1714 to 1727—Byng, Lord
Torrington—Action off Messina—Sir William Jumper—Reign of
George II., 1727 to the Treaty of Aix la Chapelle in 1748—Capture
of Portobello—Admiral Vernon—Sir Charles Wager - Sir John
Norris—Sir Peter Warren—George II., from the Peace of Aix la
Chapelle to his death in 1760—The Seven Years' War—Admiral
John Byng, his Trial and Execution—Taking of Quebec—Destruc-
tion of the French Fleet in Quiberon Bay—George III., from his
Accession to the Peace of Paris in 1763—Successes in the West
Indies—Actions with the Spanish—Admiral Boscawen—Hawke—
Lord Anson, and others.

CHAPTER VII.—George III., 1763 to 1783—Progress of Dis-
covery—Byron—Captain Cook—War of American Revolution War
with France—War with Spain—War with Holland—Siege of Gib-
raltar—Barrington—Keppel—Rodney— Kempenfelt — Loss of the
Royal George—Sir John Moore—Maurice Suckling—Sir Charles
Hardy—Sir Hyde Parker—Paul Jones.

CHAPTER VIII.—George III., 1783 to the Peace of Amiens,
1802—First War of the French Revolution—Sidney Smith at Toulon
—Lord Hood at Corsica—Horatio Nelson—Howe's Victory of the
First of June—Lord Bridport at L'Orient—Blanche and Pique—
Sidney Smith taken prisoner—Nelson at Elba—Successes in the
East and West Indies—Keith Elphinstone at the Cape—Mutiny at
Spithead and the Nore—St. Vincent—Camperdown—Cadiz—Santa
Cruz—The Nile—Acre—The Baltic—Saumarez in the Mediter-
ranean—Peace—Lord Howe—Lord St. Vincent—Sir Sidney Smith—
Lord Duncan.

CHAPTER IX.—Memoir of Lord Nelson.

CHAPTER X. — George III., from 1806 to 1820—The French
still humbled at Sea—Bombardment of Copenhagen— Detached

8, Lovell's Court, Paternoster Row, London.

Actions—War with the United States—Criticism on the American Accounts—Peace—George IV., 1820 to 1830—William IV.,—1830 to 1837—Victoria, 1837 to 1848—Collingwood—Cochrane—Troubridge — Hood — Bridport — Exmouth — Codrington — Stopford Napier.

CHAPTER XI.—The Modern British Navy.

30. **MEMORABLE WOMEN**: The Story of their Lives. By Mrs. NEWTON CROSSLAND. Eight Illustrations by BIRKET FOSTER. Fifth Edition.

"............ How to live
And how to die, forms the great question still."

Contents—Rachel Wriothesley—Lady Russell—Madame d'Arblay and Mrs. Piozzi—Mary L. Ware—Mrs. Hutchinson and Lady Fanshawe—Margaret Fuller, Marchesa Ossoli—Lady Sale.

31. **THE MISSIONARY IN MANY LANDS**: A Series of Interesting Sketches of Missionary Life and Labours, and of the Progress of the Gospel in Foreign Countries. By ERWIN HOUSE, A.M. Illustrated and Enlarged.

Contents—The Ship Duff and her Voyage—A Long Night of Toil—The Pioneers in Bengal—Then and Now in New Zealand—The Cannibals of Fiji — Eighteen Months in a Death-prison—Christian Martyrs of Madagascar—The Island Orphan Brothers.

32. **INTERESTING CHAPTERS IN SCRIPTURE HISTORY AND BIBLE ILLUSTRATION**, comprising the Literary History, Unity, Science, Agriculture, and Natural History of the Bible, &c. Illustrated and Enlarged.

Contents—Literary History of the Bible—The First entire Protestant English Version of the Bible—The Unity of Holy Scripture —The Science of the Scriptures—The Scriptural Objection to the Science of Geology Considered—Ancient Religions—The Lost Tribes of Israel—Adoption—Crucifixion—Nineveh and its Remains—Tyre —Petra, the Long-Lost Capital of Edom—The Church in the Catacombs—Illustrations of Scripture—The Agriculture of the Bible—The Ancient Cedars of Lebanon—The Serpent of the Bible—Locusts—Camels—Dogs in Eastern Cities.

33. **THE HELPING HAND**: A Guide to the New Testament. BY ADELAIDE ALEXANDER. Illustrated and Enlarged.

"The entrance of Thy words giveth light, and giveth understanding unto the simple."

34. **THE EVIDENCES OF CHRISTIANITY IN THEIR EXTERNAL DIVISION**. Concisely and popularly set forth. By CHARLES P. MCILVAINE, D.D. Edited by Dr. OLINTHUS GREGORY. Eight Illustrations.

Contents—Introductory Observations—Authenticity and Integrity of the New Testament—Credibility of the Gospel History—Argument from Miracles—Argument from Prophecy—Divine Authority of Christianity from its Propagation—Argument from its Fruits—Inspiration and Divine Authority of the Scriptures.

8, Lovell's Court, Paternoster Row, London.

35. **OUR EXEMPLARS, POOR AND RICH**; or, Biographical Sketches of Men and Women who have, by an extraordinary use of their opportunities, benefited their fellow-creatures. Edited by M. D. HILL, Recorder of Birmingham. With a preface by LORD BROUGHAM. Eight Illustrations.

Contents—The Earl of Shaftesbury—Jacques Jasmin—John Bunyan—The King of Portugal—Bridget Burke—Sister Nathalie—Rosa Governo—Francoise Caysac—Louisa Schepler—Christopher Thomson—Sir Henry Havelock—Joseph Tuckerman, D.D.—Robert Stephenson—Edmund Burke—Dr. Chalmers—David Livingstone—Hugh Miller—Christopher Columbus—The Earl of Derby—Dr. John Thomson—Harriet Ryan—Captain Machonochie—Catherine Wilkinson—John Smeaton—Frédéric Auguste Demets—The Vicomte Brétignières de Courteilles—Paul Louis Verdier—Sarah P. Remond—Sarah Martin—Sir Rowland Hill—Sir Jamsetjee Jejeebhoy—Lady Noel Brown.

36. **LECTURES TO YOUNG MEN ON VARIOUS IMPORTANT SUBJECTS**, and Gems of Thought. By HENRY WARD BEECHER. With Portrait and Illustrations.

Contents—Industry and Idleness—Twelve Causes of Dishonesty—Six Warnings—The Portrait Gallery—Gamblers and Gambling—The Strange Woman—Popular Amusements—Relative Duties—Gems of Thought.

37. **LIFE THOUGHTS.** First and Second Series complete. By HENRY WARD BEECHER. With copious Index and portrait.

38. **LEAVES FROM THE BOOK OF NATURE.** By M. S. DE VERE. With preface by THOMAS DICK, LL.D.

Contents—Only a Pebble—Nature in Motion—The Ocean and its Life—A chat about Plants—Younger years of a Plant—Later years of a Plant—Plant-Mummies—Unknown Tongues—A Trip to the Moon.

39. **WONDERS OF THE DEEP.** In Earth, Sea, Rock, and River. By M. S. DE VERE. Companion to "Leaves from the Book of Nature."

Contents—Fable and Facts—Odd Fish—Pearls—Corals—The Knight in Armour—A Pinch of Salt—Mine Oyster—Light at Sea—Light-House Stories—A Grain of Sand—Mercury—The Earth in Trouble.

40. **CHOICE TALES** By. T. S. ARTHUR. Portrait and other Illustrations.

Contents—The Widow's Son—The Reclaimed—The Drunkard's Wife—The Moderate Drinker—The Broken Merchant—The Man with the Poker—The Drunkard's Bible—After To-day—Signing the Pledge.

41. **THE YOUNG CHRISTIAN**; or, A Familiar Illustration of the Principles of Christian Duty. By JACOB ABBOTT.

Contents—I. Confession—II. The Friend—III. Prayer—IV. Consequences of Neglecting Duty—V. Almost a Christian—VI. Difficulties in Religion—VII. Evidences of Christianity—VIII. Study of the Bible—IX. The Sabbath—X. Trial and Discipline—XI. Personal Improvement—XII. Conclusion.

THE LIBRARY OF EXCELLENT LITERATURE.

Fcap. 8vo, cloth, 1s. 6d., or extra gilt edges, 2s. each.

1. **THE FRIENDS OF CHRIST IN THE NEW TESTAMENT**; or, Faith and Love Exemplified in the Lives of those who befriended Him when on Earth. By the Rev. Dr. ADAMS.

    Contents—The Wise Men from the East—Simeon—John the Baptist—The Bridegroom and Bride at Cana—The Twelve Apostles—The Children in the Temple—The Woman with the Alabaster Box—Martha and Mary—Simon the Syrenian—The Penitent Thief—The Relenting Crucifier—Joseph of Arimathea—The Women at the Sepulchre.

2. **THE BELIEVER'S JOURNEY AND FUTURE HOME IN THE BETTER LAND.** By the Rev. A. C. THOMPSON. With a Preface by the Rev. W. ARCHER, London.

    Contents—The Pilgrimage—Clustor of Eshcol—Waymarks—Glimpses of the Land—The Passage—Recognition of Friends—The Heavenly Banquet—Children in Heaven—Society of Angels—Society of the Saviour—Heavenly Honours and Riches—No Tears in Heaven—Holiness in Heaven—Activity in Heaven—The Resurrection Body—Perpetuity of Bliss in Heaven.

3. **FAMILY PRAYERS FOR EVERY MORNING AND EVENING IN THE MONTH.** With Supplementary forms of Prayer for private use &c. By the Rev. J. RAVEN, M.A.

4. **SELECT READINGS FOR USE IN DOMESTIC WORSHIP.** The Gospels of St. Matthew and St. Mark, with brief Practical Annotations. By the Rev. J. RAVEN, M.A.

5. **THE ROUGH WIND STAYED**, and other Papers. By the Rev. W. J. BROCK, B.A., late Incumbent of Hayfield, Derbyshire.

    Contents—The Rough Wind Stayed—Elijah at Horeb—The Eagle stirring up her Nest—The swelling of Jordan—The Just suffering for the Unjust—The Sympathy of Christ—The Throne of Grace—Peace the result of Confidence in God—The Glorious Gospel—Meetness for the Heavenly Inheritance—Departed Believers—The Cloud upon the Throne—The Old Paths.

6. **THE BRIGHT LIGHT IN THE CLOUD**, and other Meditations. By the Rev. W. J. BROCK. Author of "The Rough Wind Stayed."

    Contents—The Bright Light in the Clouds—Man's Frailty Contrasted with God's Word—The Ten Lepers Cleansed—Lot's Wife—The Dark Mountains—Self-examination—The Little Flock—Christ Weeping over Jerusalem—Jesus Entering Jerusalem in Triumph—The Offering of Christ—The Tranfiguration of Christ—The Conqueror from Bozrah—Redeeming the Time.

TWO-SHILLING SERIES.

Cloth, 2s., or gilt edges, side, and back, 2s. 6d.

1. **THE RELIGION OF GEOLOGY AND ITS CONNECTED SCIENCES.** By EDWARD HITCHCOCK, D.D. Cheap and Complete Edition.

2. **THE HAND OF GOD IN HISTORY;** or, Divine Providence Historically Illustrated in the Extension and Establishment of Christianity. By HOLLIS READ, A.M. With Continuation and Preface by Rev. Dr. CUMMING, F.R.S.E.

    Contents—General Illustrations of Providential Agency—Art of Printing—The Reformation—Japheth in the Tents of Shem—God in History—God in Modern Missions—Hand of God in Facilities and Resources by which to Spread Christianity—The Field Prepared—Mohammedan Countries and Mohammedanism—Hand of God in the Turkish Empire—Africa the Land of Paradoxes—The Americans—The Jews—The Nestorians—Europe in 1848—Remarkable Providences, &c.

3. **THE PLANETARY AND STELLAR WORLDS:** A Popular Exposition of the Great Discoveries and Theories of Modern Astronomy. By Professor MITCHELL. With Additions and Preface by J. GLAISHER, Greenwich Observatory. Twenty-one Illustrations.

    Contents—An Exposition of the Problem which the Heavens present for Solution—The Discoveries of the Primitive Ages—Explanation of the Motions of the Heavenly Bodies—Discovery of the Great Laws of Motion and Gravitation—Universal Gravitation applied to the Explanation of the Phenomena of the Solar System—The Stability of the Planetary System—The Discovery of the New Planets—The Cometary Worlds—The Scale on which the Universe is Built—The Motions and Revolutions of the Fixed Stars—Recent Discoveries.

4. **WANDERINGS OF A PILGRIM IN THE SHADOW OF MONT BLANC AND THE JUNGFRAU ALP.** By Rev. Dr. CHEEVER. With Corrections and Preface by Rev. J. STOUGHTON.

6. **BOGATZKY'S GOLDEN TREASURY FOR THE CHILDREN OF GOD,** consisting of Devotional and Practical Observations for every day in the Year.

7. **SAUL OF TARSUS;** The Pharisee, the Convert, the Apostle, and the Martyr. By Rev. THORNLEY SMITH. Illustrated.

8, Lovell's Court, Paternoster Row, London.

James Blackwood & Co., Publishers,

8. **LIFE AND DARING EXPLOITS OF LORD DUNDONALD.**

   Contents—Ancestry and Early Days—Early Cruises—Training in Seamanship—A Fruitless Expedition—Cruise of the "Speedy," A Career of Captures—On Shore without Employment—Afloat again, a Rich Harvest of Prizes—Enters Parliament—Cruise of the "Imperieuse"—Cochrane stands a Siege—The Basque Roads—Cochrane's Plan of Attack — A Singular Imprisonment — The Stock Exchange Trial—Fighting once more, but under a Foreign Flag—Closing Years of Repose and Redress.

9. **TRUE STORIES OF THE TIMES OF RICHARD II.** Illustrating the History, Manners and Customs of that King's reign. By Rev. H. P. DUNSTER, M.A. With Illustrations.

   Contents—Berwick Castle—The Battle at the Church of Nevele—Wat Tyler's Rebellion—Singular Adventure of the Earl of Flanders The Passage of the River Lis—The Surprise of Oudenarde—The Tilt—Deep Scheme of the Duke of Brittany—The Lost Pennon—Grand Doings at Paris—Two Heads better than One; or, the Castle of Ventadour—The Famous Tournament of St. Inglevere—Narrow Escape of Sir Oliver de Clisson, Constable of France—A Masked Dance at the French Court—King Richard's Irish Expedition—The Challenge—Flint Castle; or, the King's Greyhound—Coronation of the Duke of Lancaster—The Death and Funeral of King Richard II.

10. **STORIES FOR ALL READERS.** By Rev. J. YOUNG, M.A.

    "Real life has extravagances that would not be admitted to appear in a well-written romance, they would be said to be out of Nature."—*Cecil's Memoirs of Newton.*

    Contents—The Brothers—The Separation—A Providential Journey—Lake Erie—Results—A Tale of the Kremlin—The Alibi—A Modern Xantippi—The Slave Trade—The Village Clergyman—The Conscientious Hair Dresser—The Genuine Philosopher—The Triumph of Feeling—Changes.

11. **ORNAMENTS DISCOVERED.** Illustrated.

12. **MAMA'S NEW BIBLE STORIES FROM THE OLD AND NEW TESTAMENTS.** By EMILY G. NESBITT. With Eight Illustrations.

    Contents—OLD TESTAMENT.—Lot—The Good Servant—Rahab—Jericho—Ai—The Story-Tellers, &c.—Gideon—Lamps and Pitchers—The First King—David's Sin—The Undutiful Son—Solomon's Temple—Rehoboam—The Mother and Child—The Good King—The Uncle and Aunt—The Wicked King and Queen—The Two Friends—More about Ahab—Another Good King.

8, Lovell's Court, Paternoster Row, London.

NEW TESTAMENT.—John the Baptist—King Herod—Cleansing the Leper—The Storm at Sea—The Ruler's Daughter—The Widow's Son—Blind Bartimeus—Purifying the Temple—The Widow's Mite—The Last Supper—Peter's Denial—The Holy Spirit—Ananias and Sapphira—The First Martyr.

PARABLES.—The Lord and His Husbandmen—The Sower—The Ten Virgins—The Two Houses—The Unmerciful Servant—The Prodigal Son.

13. **ELM GRANGE**; or, A Summer in the Country. By E. A. M. Eight Illustrations.

Contents—Going into the Country—The Journey—The Arrival—The Nursery—Cowslips—The Cuckoo—Hill End—The Farmyard—The Rabbits—Master Willie—Malvern—The Sunday Morning after—Hay-Making—Dinner in the Hay-Field—Going Home.

14. **THOUGHTS FOR THE THOUGHTLESS AND THE THOUGHTFUL**; or, Inducements for Scientific Inquiry. By Mrs. C. H. SMITH. Numerous Illustrations.

Contents—Introductory Chapter—The Atmosphere—On the Earth—On Water—The Vegetable Kingdom—The Animal Kingdom—The Celestial System—Conclusion.

15. **THE PILGRIM'S PROGRESS FROM THIS WORLD TO THAT WHICH IS TO COME.** By JOHN BUNYAN. With Explanatory Notes. By Rev. W. MASON and others, and a Life of the Author. With Numerous Illustrations.

16. **THE SEVEN CHAMPIONS OF CHRISTENDOM.** With Eight Illustrations.

17. **TRAVELS, VOYAGES, AND ADVENTURES IN STRANGE COUNTRIES AND FOREIGN PARTS.** By PETER PARLEY. Eight Illustrations.

18. **PEARLS OF SHAKSPEARE**: a Collection of the most brilliant passages found in his plays. Illustrated by KENNY MEADOWS.

19. **ORATIONS, LECTURES, AND ESSAYS.** By RALPH WALDO EMERSON.

8, Lovell's Court, Paternoster Row, London.

BOOKS FOR YOUNG PERSONS.

...ted and handsomely bound, gilt edges, imperial 16mo, square, 3s. 6d. each.

PARLOUR PASTIMES, a Repertoire of acting Charades, Fireside Games, Enigmas, Riddles, Charades, Conundrums, Arithmetical and Mechanical Puzzles, Parlour Magic, &c. Numerous Illustrations.

is a delightful book for the young, and calculated to render home happy.

Contents—Acting Charades—Pantomime Charades—Dialogue Charades—Tableaux Vivants—The Magic Lantern—Fireside Games—Enigmas—Charades—Logogriphs—Arithmetical Puzzles—Mechanical Puzzles—Conundrums—Transpositions—Anagrams—Rebuses—Parlour Magic—Curiosities of Science—The Secret of Ventriloquism.

GAMES FOR ALL SEASONS: Consisting of In-door and Out-door Sports, Athletic Exercises, Fireside Amusements for Winter Evenings, Chess, Draughts, Backgammon, Riddles, Puzzles, Conundrums, Magic and Legerdemain, Fireworks, &c., &c. Numerous Illustrations. A Sequel to "Parlour Pastimes."

General Contents.—Out-door Games: Cricket—Croquet—Parlour Croquet—Troco, or Lawn Billiards—Red, White, and Blue—Aunt Sally—Jack's Alive—Skittle Games—Aquatic Sports—Minor Outdoor Sports—Archery—Gymnastics. In-door Amusements: Chess—Magic and Mystery—Fireworks—Domestic Pets—The Riddler—Forfeits—Little Fortune-Teller—The Magic of the Ancients—The Portable Diorama—Foot Ball.

THE FROST KING; or, The Power of Kindness, and how it Prevailed over Fear and Cruelty. Illustrated.

Contents—The Frost King; or, The Power of Kindness—Eva's Visit to Fairy Land—Lily Bell and Thistle Down—Little Bud—Little Sunbeam's Song of Clover Blossom—Little Annie's Dream—Star Twinkle; or, The Flower's Lessons on Humility—The May Day Festival—The Voice of the Wind—Ripple, the Water Spirit—Fairy Song.

...OY; or, New Drawing Room Charades for Home Performance. By ANNEMINA DE YOUNGE. Illustrated.

Contents — Mis(s)-for-tune — For-give — Ring-let — Com(c)-fort—Plain-tiff—Off-ice—Mess-age—The Sleeping Beauty—Love under a Mask—New Year's Eve.

Lovell's Court, Paternoster Row, London.

BOOKS FOR YOUNG PERSONS.

Illustrated and handsomely bound, gilt edges, imperial 16mo, square, 2s. 6d. each.

1. **HAPPY HOURS AT WYNFORD GRANGE**: A Story for Children. By CUTHBERT BEDE. Four Coloured Illustrations.

    Contents—Eleanor Wynford—The Young Architect—The Nursery at Wynford Grange—Games and Lessons—A Holiday Walk—Calling upon Friends — The Doll's Tea Party — An Evening's Pleasure—Christmas Characters—The Child's Costume Ball—The Christmas Tree—All things come to an end.

2. **AUNT DOROTHY'S STORY-BOOK FOR A GOOD CHILD, A NAUGHTY CHILD, AND A MEDDLESOME MATTY.** By MARY and ELIZABETH KIRBY. Four Illustrations.

    Contents—Ellen's Holiday—The Golden Gates—The Selfish Boy—The Mysterious Letter.

3. **THE LITTLE SILVER BARREL**, and other Tales. By PAUL MUSSET. Illustrations.

    Contents—The Little Silver Barrel—Mabel, and her Fairy Friends—The Adventures of Peter Pry—The Three Wishes.

4. **THE BOOK OF SPORTS FOR BOYS AND GIRLS.** Containing Games, Recreations, and Amusements for the Play Room and Play Ground, at Home or at School. By WILLIAM MARTIN. Numerous Illustrations.

    Contents—Games with Marbles—Games for Cold Weather—Dangerous Games—Gymnastics—Cricket—Swimming—Gardening—Carpentering—Keeping Poultry—Bees.

5. **VESSELS AND VOYAGES**, a Book for Boys. By UNCLE GEORGE. Numerous Illustrations.

6. **OLD TESTAMENT HISTORY FOR YOUNG PERSONS.** By INGRAM COBBIN, M.A.

8, Lovell's Court, Paternoster Row, London.

CHOICE BOOKS FOR YOUNG PERSONS.

1s. each, cloth, Illustrated.

1. Bright Gems for the Young. A Collection of Little Stories with Great Meanings.
2. Sparkling Gems: Being Short Stories for the benefit of Young People.
3. Bright Diamonds, Set in Short Stories for the Young.
4. Sparkling Diamonds, in Lessons for Young Readers.
5. The Sacred Mountains. By Rev. J. T. HEADLEY.
6. The Fountain of Living Waters.
7. Sacred Scenes and Characters. By Rev. J. T. HEADLEY.
8. Gutenberg and the Lost Child.
9. The Little Shoemaker; or, Where the Truth takes Root God will make of it a Goodly Tree.
10. Hugh Fisher; or, Home Principles.
11. Patient Waiting, No Loss. By Cousin ALICE.
12. No Such Word as Fail. By Cousin ALICE.
13. Contentment Better than Wealth. By Cousin ALICE.
14. The Sacred Plains. By Rev. J. T. HEADLEY.
15. The Successful Boy; or, The Duties of Masters and Apprentices Illustrated and Enforced.
16. The Widow's Sixpence.
17. Annandale. A Tale of the Scottish Covenanters.
18. Ten Nights in a Bar Room. A Temperance Tale. By T. S. ARTHUR.
19. The Basket of Flowers.
20. History of Susan Gray. By Mrs. SHERWOOD.
21. The Phenomena of the Four Seasons. By Professor HITCHCOCK.

Series to be continued.

READINGS FOR YOUNG PERSONS.

Foolscap 8vo, cloth, 1s. each, Illustrated.

1. The Widow's Son. By T. S. ARTHUR.
2. The Drunkard's Wife. By T. S. ARTHUR.
3. The Broken Merchant. By T. S. ARTHUR.
4. The Lighted Way.
5. Learning better than House.

8, Lovell's Court, Paternoster Row, London.

USEFUL WORKS.

1. **TAKE MY ADVICE**; A Book for Every Home, giving complete and Trustworthy Information on everything pertaining to Daily Life. Crown 8vo, cloth, Illustrated, price 2s. 6d., 360 pp.

    Contents—Household Management—Domestic Cookery—Brewing and Distilling—Domestic Medicine—Domestic Chemistry—Clothing Garden Management—Law of Agreements, Leases, I O U's, Bills of Exchange, &c.—Trade, Artistic, and Scientific Facts—Etiquette and Manners — In-door and Out-door Games—Domestic Pets—Domestic Pests—Ladies Work—Something for Everybody—and other matters. By the late Editor of the Family Friend.

    ** *This is one of the most complete books of the kind ever offered to the Public, and published at an unusually low price.*

2. **THE BOOK OF DATES**; or, Treasury of Universal Reference, comprising the principal Events in All Ages, from the Earliest Records to the Present Time. With Index of Events and Numerous Tables of Permanent Interest to the Student. Demy 8vo, cloth, price 10s. 6d., more than 800 pages of closely printed matter.

3. **A COMPLETE PRACTICAL GUIDE TO HER MAJESTY'S CIVIL SERVICE**; containing in full the Examination Papers for every Department used since the Appointment of the Commissioners; Full Details of the Limits of Age and Qualifications of Candidates; Hints to Candidates for every Office; and Copious Tables of the Emoluments and Superannuation Allowances of every Civil Servant in Great Britain, Ireland, India, and the Colonies. By a Certificated Candidate, an Officer of Her Majesty's Civil Service. Crown 8vo, cloth, 2s. 6d.

4. **THE MANSE GARDEN**; or, Plain Instructions in the Pleasant Culture of Fruit Trees, Flowers, Vegetables, and Sweet Herbs, for the Beauty and Profit of the Villa or Farm. By NATHANIEL PATERSON, D.D. Fifteenth Thousand. Crown 8vo, cloth, 2s.

    This is a complete and practical guide for gardening in all departments. It is divided into three parts, viz., Forest and Fruit Trees, Vegetables and Sweet Herbs, and Flowers, on all of which such instructions are given as can be easily carried out. This work also contains a *select* list of trees and flowers, a list of hardy, half hardy, and tender annuals, biennials, perennials, alphabetical list of particular flowers, monthly summary of gardening work in season, &c. &c.

8, Lovell's Court, Paternoster Row, London.

5. **READINGS FOR YOUNG MEN, MERCHANTS, AND MEN OF BUSINESS**, containing numerous Maxims, Truisms, and Articles on Probity and the Management of Business on Sound and Honourable Principles. Crown 8vo, cloth, 1s. 6d.

6. **CŒLEBS IN SEARCH OF A COOK**; with Divers Receipts and other Delectable Things relating to the Gastronomic Art. Crown 8vo, cloth, 2s.

   Contents.—In Search of a Cook—On the Principle and Practice of Eating and Drinking—Income and Expenditure—Station in Life—Choice of Company—Conduct during Dinner—Breakfasts—Luncheons and Suppers, and Bills of Fare and Receipts for Fifty-three Different Dinners, &c.

7. **GESENIUS' HEBREW GRAMMAR.** Translated without Abridgment, by T. J. CONANT, Professor of Hebrew in the Literary and Theological Institution at Hamilton, New York, with a Course of Exercises and a Hebrew Chrestomathy, by the Translator. A New Edition. Royal 8vo, cloth, 5s.

8. **THE BROAD LINE DRAWING-BOOK**, for the use of Young Beginners, containing nearly One Hundred Drawings of Objects. Sixth Thousand. Cloth, 2s. 6d.

   Ditto, ditto, in Five Parts, each complete and sold separately, with covers printed in gold, 6d. each.

9. **BLACKWOOD'S SHILLING ATLAS**; containing 13 Maps, corrected up to the Present Time. Coloured. Copious Index and handsome Wrapper printed in Colours, royal 4to, making it the most elegant and complete Atlas ever issued at the price. 1s.

10. **BLACKWOOD'S HAND ATLAS**; containing 12 Maps, Coloured. Royal 8vo, 1s.

11. **THE TEMPLES OF THE HEBREWS**: Their Courts, Sanctuaries, Furniture, and Festivals. An Epitome of the Laws, Literature, Religion, and Sacred Antiquities of the Jewish Nation. By the Rev. T. BANNISTER, LL.D. Crown 8vo, 7s. 6d.

12. **THE INFALLIBLE READY-RECKONER.** With Complete Interest Tables, and much Useful Information. By W. COXHEAD. 18mo, cloth, 1s.

6, Lovell's Court, Paternoster Row, London.

MISCELLANEOUS.

1. **MANNERS AND CUSTOMS OF THE ENGLISH NATION**, from the Earliest Period to the Present Time. Cloth, Illustrated. 5s.
2. **THE CURATE OF INVERESK**: A Clerical Autobiography. By BRACEBRIDGE HEMYNG. Crown 8vo, cloth. 5s.
3. **THE SEVEN SISTERS OF SLEEP**: A Popular History of the Seven Prevailing Narcotics of the World. By M. C. COOKE, Director of the Metropolitan Scholastic Museum. Crown 8vo, cloth, Illust. 7s. 6d.
4. **THE PROGRESS OF SCIENCE, ART, AND LITERATURE IN RUSSIA.** By F. R. GRAHAME. Crown 8vo, cloth. 7s. 6d.
5. **ARMINIUS**; or, The History of the German People and their Legal and Constitutional Customs, from the days of Julius Cæsar to the days of Charlemagne. By the late THOMAS SMITH, F.S.A. Edited by his Son. Crown 8vo, cloth. 10s. 6d.
6. **THE APPLICATION OF PROPHECY TO THE CRIMEAN WAR**; or, From the Accession of Louis Napoleon to the Throne of France to the Present and Future Times. By G. B. HILDEBRAND. Crown 8vo, cloth. 5s.
7. **LIFE AND WORK OF ST. PAUL**, Practically Considered and Applied. By ALEXANDER ROBERTS, D.D. 5s.
8. **THE QUEEN'S PARDON.** By MARY EYRE. 5s.
9. **THE YOUTH'S BIBLE AND COMMENTATOR**: Being the Holy Scriptures written in a Simple and Attractive Manner for the Young. By INGRAM COBBIN, M.A. A New Edition, Revised and Corrected, with Numerous Illustrations, &c. Imperial, gilt edges, extra cloth. 7s. 6d.
10. **PRACTICAL HYDROPATHY** (Not the Cold-Water System). Including plans of Baths, and Remarks on Diet, Clothing, and Habits of Life; with Simple Directions how to carry out the Treatment at Home, and to meet sudden attacks of Disease or Accidents. Illustrated with 160 Anatomical Engravings, Plans of Baths, &c. By JOHN SMEDLEY. Crown 8vo. 2s. 6d.
11. **LADIES' MANUAL OF PRACTICAL HYDROPATHY** (Not the Cold-Water System). With various new External Applications; also Directions how to carry out the Treatment for Children and Adults, &c., &c. By Mrs. SMEDLEY. Cloth. 2s.

8, Lovell's Court, Paternoster Row, London.

LIBRARY OF FICTION AND HUMOUR.

Small post 8vo, Illustrated, 3s. 6d. cloth, each.

1. **THE ADVENTURES OF MR. VERDANT GREEN**, an Oxford Freshman. By CUTHBERT BEDE, B.A. With Hundreds of Illustrations drawn by the Author. One Hundred and Seventh Thousand. Crown 8vo.
   "A college joke to cure the dumps."

2. **HUMOUR, WIT, AND SATIRE.** By CUTHBERT BEDE, B.A., Author of "Verdant Green." Crown 8vo.

3. **THE WORLD IN LIGHT AND SHADE:** Its Comicalities and Eccentricities. By ALFRED W. COLE.

4. **LEGENDS IN PROSE AND VERSE.** Humorous, Serious, Sarcastic, Sentimental, and Supernatural. By ALFRED W. COLE. Illustrations by HARVEY.

5. **MISS BROWN:** A Romance; and other Tales. By R. B. BROUGH. Numerous Illustrations.

6. **LITTLE MR. BOUNCER AND HIS FRIEND MR. VERDANT GREEN.** By CUTHBERT BEDE, B.A. With numerous Illustrations by the Author. 2s. 6d.

8. Lovell's Court, Paternoster Row, London.

BLACKWOOD'S LONDON LIBRARY.

Fcap. 8vo, Coloured Wrappers, 2s. each.

SUITABLE FOR RAILWAY READING.

1. Living for Appearances. A Tale. By the Brothers MAYHEW. Illustrated by M'CONNELL.
2. The Two Brothers; or, The Family that Lived in the First Society. By M. RAVEN.
3. The Ghost-Seer. By SCHILLER.
4. Hargrave; or, The Adventures of a Man of Fashion. By Mrs. TROLLOPE.
5. The Robertses on their Travels. By Mrs. TROLLOPE.
6. The Three Cousins. By Mrs. TROLLOPE.
7. Men of Capital. By Mrs. GORE.
8. Preferment. By Mrs. GORE.
9. The Man About Town. By CORNELIUS WEBBE.
10. The Absent Man. By CORNELIUS WEBBE.
11. De Clifford; or, The Constant Man.
12. The Mysterious Parchment. By Rev. J. WAKEMAN.
13. The Captain's Daughter.
14. How I Tamed Mrs. Cruiser. By GEO. AUGUSTUS SALA.
15. Tales from the Operas.
16. The Ticket-of-Leave Man.
18. Lorimer Littlegood, Esq., a Young Gentleman who wished to see Society, and Saw it accordingly.
19. Sea-Drift. By Vice-Admiral ROBINSON.
20. Fair and False.
21. The Fortunes of the House of Pennyl.
22. Wanderings of a Pilgrim. By Dr. CHEEVER.
23. Confessions of a Horse-Dealer.
24. Miss Brown. A Romance. By BROUGH.
25. The Male Flirt; or, Ladies Beware of Him. By Mrs. GORDON SMYTHIES.
26. The Minstrel and the Maid of Kent. By CAPTAIN CURLING.
27. The Mariner's Compass.

8, Lovell's Court, Paternoster Row, London.

...wood & Co., Publishers,   29

... By Percy B. St. John.

... By Admiral Robinson.
... By Mrs. Holmes.

... Life and Character.
... : A Country Ghost Story.

... FOR RAILWAY READING.

... of Mrs. Partington. 1s.
... of Beauty. By Cuthbert Bede, B.A. 1s.
... and other Matters. By Alf. W. Cole.

... Caught in His Own Trap. 6d.

... ...onal Songs. 1s.

SPELLINGS.

..., 6d. each. Cloth, Rims, 1s. each.

| Carpenter. | Dilworth. |
| Fenning. | Markham. |

...'s Court, Paternoster Row, London.

BLACKWOOD'S DIARIES.

(All the matter in these Diaries is Copyright.)

The following DIARIES, published yearly in October, are printed on cream paper; all information officially corrected. They are issued with the conviction that they are the very best in the market at the prices affixed :—

1. "Blackwood's Shilling Scribbling Diary." Seven days on each page, interleaved with Blotting Paper. 1s. fcap, folio, Size 13 by 8¼ inches.
2. Blackwood's Three-Day Diary. Three Days on each page. Price 1s. 6d. Size 13 by 8¼ inches.
3. The same, interleaved with Blotting Paper, 2s.
4. Blackwood's Desk Diary No. 4. Seven Days on each page. Large 8vo, 1s. bound in cloth. Size 8¼ by 5¼ inches.
5. Blackwood's Larger Desk Diary No. 5. Three Days on each page. Large 8vo, 2s. bound in cloth. Size 8¼ by 5¼ inches.
5. The same Diary, with Blotting Paper, 2s. 6d.
6. Blackwood's Foolscap 8vo Diary No. 6. Seven Days on each page, interleaved with Blotting Paper. 1s. bound in cloth. Size 6¾ by 4¼ inches.
7. Blackwood's Larger Foolscap 8vo Diary No. 7. Three Days on each page. 1s. bound in cloth. Size 6½ by 4¼ inches.
7. The same Diary, with Blotting Paper, 1s. 6d.
8. Blackwood's Tablet. Seven Days on each Sheet, to be torn off or turned over at the end of each week when used. 1s.
9. Blackwood's Quarto Diary. Three Days to each page, ruled feint only, stiff cover, cloth back, 1s. 6d. Size 10 by 8 inches.
9. The same, interleaved with Blotting Paper, 2s.
10. Blackwood's Pocket Book and Diary for Gentlemen. Illustrated, roan tuck, or elastic band, 1s.
11. Blackwood's Pocket Book and Diary for Ladies. Containing appropriate and original information. Illustrated, roan tuck, or elastic band, 1s.
12. Blackwood's National Pocket Book and Diary. Illustrated, roan tuck, or elastic band, 1s.

8, Lovell's Court, Paternoster Row, London.

James Blackwood & Co., Publishers,

Blackwood's Small Pocket Book and Diary. Roan tuck, limp or elastic band, 6d.

The same, in paper covers, 4d.

Blackwood's Large Pocket Book and Diary. Fcap. 8vo, roan tuck or elastic band, 2s. 6d.

Blackwood's Pocket Book and Diary for Gentlemen. Paper covers, 6d.

Blackwood's Pocket Book and Diary for Ladies. Paper covers, 6d.

Blackwood's National Pocket Book and Diary. Paper covers, 6d.

Perpetual Slate Tablet Diary. With moveable days and months, and Slate Tablet for weekly memoranda. In wooden glass case, "A most useful article." 5s.

Registered Perpetual Remembrancer. Containing moveable Monthly Diary, moveable Days of Months and Weeks. In wooden glass-case, 5s. "Indispensable for the counting-house."

All these Diaries are printed on good paper, well bound, and will be found unequalled in price and usefulness.

A permanent cloth cover may be had for Numbers 1, 2, and 3, price 1s. 4d. each.

www.ingramcontent.com/pod-product-compliance
Lightning Source LLC
Chambersburg PA
CBHW031446160426
43195CB00010BB/868